On Guard!

Seven Safeguards to Protect Your Sexual Purity

GARY AND JOY LUNDBERG

Published and distributed by
Riverpark Publishing Co.

Distribution office:
Riverpark Publishing Co.
3680 N. Little Rock Drive
Provo, Ut 84604
801-224-3447

Printed in the United States of America

1 2 3 4 5 6 7 8 9 0

Library of Congress Control Number: 2002090733
ISBN 0-915029-05-7

Salt Lake Temple wedding photo by Massey Studios
Washington D.C. wedding photo by Photographic Services

On Guard!

Seven Safeguards to Protect Your Sexual Purity

Other books by Gary and Joy Lundberg

Married for Better, Not Worse

I Don't Have to Make Everything All Better

On Guard!

Seven Safeguards to Protect Your Sexual Purity

CONTENTS

INTRODUCTION

We think the youth and young adults of the Church are terrific. They want to do what's right. This was overwhelmingly confirmed when we were speaking at a youth conference to over 700 teens from Idaho in a college auditorium. When we talked to them about setting dating boundaries—what to do when your date does such and such—we were blown away by their response. In the middle of our talk, as we demonstrated what to do, they jumped up and gave us an enthusiastic standing ovation.

Since then, at youth and institute firesides, morning sides for seminaries, and at other youth conferences, we have been deeply moved by the number of young people who come up to us and say, "Thank you so much. I just didn't know what to do. Now I do." Some, with tears running down their cheeks have said, "I want to do what's right. Thank you for being specific and teaching me how."

As we have talked with youth, young adults, parents, and leaders about these seven safeguards, over and over we have heard them say, "Hurry! We need the book now." Many have shared their ideas and personal stories with us, and for this we express our sincere appreciation to each of them. In most cases we have changed the names in experiences printed to protect their privacy. We want to also express our gratitude for our editor, Darla Isackson. Her talent and insights have been significantly helpful.

For ease of reading, the book is worded as though I, Joy, were the only writer; however, my husband Gary and I have written it together. His experiences as a marriage and family counselor and bishop, mine as a Relief Society president and Young Women's leader, and our combined experiences as youth teachers and parents, have helped prepare us to write this book.

Through all these opportunities to work with people we have seen firsthand the happiness of those who have chosen to be morally clean. We want all youth to experience that kind of lasting joy. We've also seen the sorrow that comes to those who lose their sexual purity, and want to help as many as possible avoid experiencing that sorrow. And we've also seen the joy of those who have repented and become worthy once again. We rejoice with them.

We have written this book to help you discover ways to guard yourself and stay morally clean and temple worthy. We don't intend for this book to replace the wise counsel of your bishop or your parents. To the contrary, we encourage you to go to them and discuss the things you read here. If you have need of repentance, go see your bishop right away and he will help you in that sacred process.

We have quoted the scriptures and statements of many of the prophets and other Church leaders whose constant desire is for the youth of the Church to enjoy the greatest happiness possible. We, too, express our love and desire for you to experience the joy that Jesus Christ has in store for you.

Now jump in with both feet, read, apply, and find that happiness.

Joy and Gary Lundberg

Safeguard #1

Understand Why Sexual Purity Is So Important

"Whoso committeth adultery . . . lacketh understanding."
–PROVERBS 6:32

Everyone enjoys receiving a gift. There's always the wonder of what's inside the package, and even if we know what it is, we feel the excitement and anticipation of using the gift. For a moment picture yourself back in the pre-existence. Heavenly Father is lovingly giving you last-minute counsel before you leave His presence to come here to earth. He hands you a beautifully wrapped gift, and says, "Honor and cherish this gift, but don't open it until your wedding day." Then He gives this warning: "Satan will try to persuade you to open it before that time. Oh, he won't do it all at once. He's too clever for that. He'll try to convince you that it's all right to play with the ribbons and even remove them, but not to pull off all the wrapping paper and open the box just yet. He knows if he can get you to untie the ribbons, and start to take off even a small part of the wrappings he'll have the power to convince you to prematurely open the gift all the way."

Then, your Father, with the most tender, caring look in His eyes, says, "I'm asking you with all the love in my heart to wait until the appointed time before you handle this gift in any way. It's your sexual purity, and if you honor it as I have asked, I promise I will give you wonderful blessings beyond your comprehension."

Though this story is allegorical, the principle is true. God has given you a sacred and beautiful gift with glorious blessings attached to it. He designed this gift to dwell within you, to be honored, cherished, and kept safely in reserve until your wedding day. And then ever after the gift is to be treated with the greatest care, to be tenderly shared only with your mate to whom you are legally married.

JUST HOW IMPORTANT IS IT?

To help you have a vision of how important this gift is, do a little more imagining with us. It's Friday night and the basketball game has ended. In the rush and excitement of the crowd you are separated from the friends you came with. They pile into their cars and off they go, unknowingly leaving you behind. No one is home to call for a ride, so you begin walking. It's a dark night and as you walk along the poorly lit street you feel uneasy. You know it's not safe to walk alone at night, but you have no choice. As you hurry along you sense that someone is coming up behind you. You turn around and see a man with a knife raised, ready to plunge it into your back.

What would you do? Would you smile at him, rub your hands together in delightful anticipation and say, "Oh, this looks exciting! I think I'll hang around and see what happens. A few little stabs won't hurt." That's completely unrealistic—no one would ever be that foolish. What *would* you do? Unless you're some kind of bionic being with the power to take the guy apart, you would run, probably scream *and* run. It's certain that you would do everything in your power to get away from the danger and save your life.

President Ezra Taft Benson said, "Guard your virtue as you would your very life."[1] In other words, whether you are a guy or a girl, if someone you are dating tries to make a move on you that would take away your virtue—your sexual purity—you would do whatever it takes to prevent that from happening, just as you would do everything you could to get away from someone trying to kill you. It's that important.

Which brings us to the question: Why *is* it so important? There are two main reasons you must protect your sexual purity with every ounce of strength and intellect you possess.

1. IT'S A COMMANDMENT FROM HEAVENLY FATHER

Throughout the scriptures the Lord has made it clear that it is wrong to be sexually immoral. Most recently He spoke through our prophets who wrote the following in *The Family: A Proclamation to the World:* "The sacred powers of procreation are to be employed only between man and woman, lawfully wedded as husband and wife."

To further clarify this issue, our leaders stated in the booklet *For the Strength of Youth,* "God has commanded that sexual intimacy be reserved for marriage."[2] The following statement by Elder Richard G. Scott helps us understand how this commandment is violated: "Any sexual intimacy outside the bonds of marriage—I mean any intentional contact with the sacred, private parts of another's body, with or without clothing—is a sin and is forbidden by God."[3]

No one need wonder where the Lord stands on the issue of morality. People may try to justify inappropriate actions with all sorts of excuses such as "It's a natural thing to do," or "I'll repent later," or "We're in love, so it's okay." One who truly loves you would never persuade you in this way, but would rather help you do all in your power to protect you from the sorrows of this sin. In the scriptures God has made it clear that to break this commandment is "most abominable above all sins save it be the shedding of innocent blood or denying the Holy Ghost" (Alma 39:5).

Why Has He Given This Commandment?

Understanding that Father in Heaven has given this commandment because He loves you and wants you to enjoy the greatest happiness possible will help you desire to obey Him. Many couples throughout the world are enjoying this promised happiness today.

Kevin and Marilee are one such couple. We witnessed the joy that surrounded them in the temple the day they were married. Marilee was beautiful in her lovely white wedding gown. Kevin, all in white too, had a look of radiant happiness on his face. After the sacred vows were spoken and their love was sealed for time and all eternity, they kissed through tears and smiles as husband and wife. This was their dream come true and those nearby could hear Marilee say, "We made it! We made it!" This is a goal all Latter-day Saints can achieve if they are determined to keep God's commandments and live morally clean lives worthy of such a glorious blessing. It is a vitally important step along the path to the Celestial Kingdom.

Now, let's look at the second reason you must protect your sexual purity with every ounce of strength and intellect you possess.

2. IT'S SMART, NOT STUPID, TO BE SEXUALLY PURE

Satan would have you believe otherwise. In an effort to justify their own evil actions misguided people try to make others feel stupid and naive for not participating in illicit sexual behavior. The media glorifies immorality, making it appear enticing, acceptable, and normal. President Gordon B. Hinckley warned that "The adversary of truth would like to injure you, would like to destroy your faith, would like to lead you down paths that are beguiling and interesting, but deadly."[4]

How Can You Stand Up to Peer Pressure?

Those who follow Satan *are* beguiling and would have you believe that not being sexually active is a sign of immaturity and abnormality.

Many—young and old—get caught up in this way of thinking and rationalizing. They then put pressure on peers to join in their self-destructive behavior.

Earl, a high school football player in Texas experienced that kind of pressure. He was not a member of the Church and knew nothing of its teachings, but was a wise young man who thoughtfully considered his options. His teammates made fun of him for not participating in immoral activities. They would laugh and say, "You're stupid. All those girls are out there just for the picking." He was not impressed nor persuaded by their comments because he had seen the unhappiness that had resulted from this type of behavior. Some of the girls who were dating his teammates would come crying to him saying they hated being sexually involved but were afraid their boyfriends wouldn't like them if they didn't do it. He tried to convince them that such a reason had no merit. They persisted in their immoral behavior.

He saw the sadness of unwanted pregnancies, venereal disease, abortion, and lack of self-respect, and determined he wanted no part of it. He had made a significantly important decision in the ninth grade. He said, "I wanted to someday marry a morally clean woman and I knew that I could expect nothing more of her than I was willing to give." He felt he owed his future wife his own sexual purity.

At the time of these experiences he didn't know it was a commandment from God to be morally clean; he just knew it was smart. It was as though he knew and understood the counsel President Hinckley has given: "Any [young man] who indulges in illegitimate sexual activity . . . does himself irreparable damage and robs her with whom he is involved of that which can never be restored. There is nothing clever about this kind of so-called conquest. It carries with it no laurels, no victories, no enduring satisfaction. It brings only shame, sorrow, and regret."[5]

In time, Earl received an athletic scholarship to Brigham Young University where he was taught the gospel, joined the Church, dated a lovely Latter-day Saint woman and married her in the temple. The decisions he had made earlier had prepared him for this single most important event in his life, and when the time came he was worthy and ready.

ARE YOU SAVVY ABOUT SEXUALLY TRANSMITTED DISEASES?

Significant evidence substantiates how smart it is to be chaste. For one thing, unchastity is dangerous to your health. Many young people don't know how seriously dangerous it is. Though the following facts and information are harsh and startling, you need to be fully aware of what can happen to those who choose to be sexually active before marriage. According to research by Pro-Life America

- Sexually active people face odds four times higher for contracting a sexually transmitted disease (STD) than for getting pregnant.
- Three million teenagers contract STDs annually.[6]

Elder Neal A. Maxwell said, "Reports indicate that 'as many as 43 million Americans may have acquired incurable sexually transmitted viral infections'."[7] HIV is one of these infections which, as you know, leads to AIDS.

According to the United States Department of Health and Human Service, those infected with STDs can experience serious damage to their bodies, including genital sores and warts, infertility, birth defects, blindness, increased risk of cancer, brain damage and even death in some cases. STDs can be passed from a mother to her child during pregnancy and/or birth, causing fetal death or an infant born with physical and mental developmental disabilities.[8]

Imagine the time when you and your future husband begin having a family and you're in the doctor's office for your prenatal exam and the doctor asks you if you have any STDs. What a relief it will be for you to be able to look him in the eye and say, with absolute assurance, "No." What a blessing that will be to you and your baby.

If caught early there are cures for bacterial STDs, but no cure for some viral STDs. Even though antibiotics can cure bacterial STDs, significant and permanent damage can result if the disease is not diagnosed and treated early. Some of these diseases are without symptoms and people often are unaware of the fact they are infected until the damage has been done.

To Be Forewarned is To Be Forearmed

After experiencing the frightening results of a sexually transmitted disease, a young woman said to her counselor, "If I had known this was going to happen to me, I would have made a different choice. But no one told me." What a tragic after-the-fact discovery. You now know what can happen.

Some justify their sexual misconduct by saying it's okay as long as they use protection. That's a frightening deception. There are men and women who are infected with STDs, wiping their tears and saying, "but we thought we were safe—we took precautions." There are many pregnant women in this world with puzzled looks on their faces, scratching their heads and saying, "but we used protection."

REPERCUSSIONS OF UNWANTED PREGNANCY

What are the results of an unwanted pregnancy? Some resort to abortion, which is one of the most shattering solutions anyone can choose. On the subject of abortion the Church has taken a very clear stand. In the *Encyclopedia of Mormonism* we read, "Members of the Church must not 'submit to, be a party to, or perform an abortion' (General Handbook, 11-4). The only exceptions are where 'incest or rape was involved, or where competent medical authorities certify that the life of the mother is in jeopardy, or that a severely defective fetus cannot survive birth' (Packer, p. 85). Even these exceptions do not justify abortion automatically. Church members are counseled that they should consider abortion in such cases only after consulting with their bishop and receiving divine confirmation through prayer."[9]

Abortion has serious spiritual, emotional, and physical repercussions. In one survey of women in the United States who had had an abortion, more than 80% said they regretted doing it.[10] Besides the haunting psychological problems that plague those who have had an abortion, it involves the possibility of serious physical consequences. A report from Pro-Life America stated, "Abortion may be legal, but it's . . . not safe. Women are injured and killed by abortion every year in America, even in some of the most prestigious hospitals."[11]

The Tragedy of Unwanted Babies

Some young unwed mothers who opt to keep and raise their babies end up experiencing problems they never dreamed they would face. Besides the tragedy of not giving their child the benefit of two loving parents, some mothers resent the child, and consequently cause psychological problems for their child and themselves. Unwed mothers usually have serious financial hardships and, according to some surveys, never rise above the national poverty level. Church leaders encourage young unwed mothers to choose adoption.

Men who have fathered these unwanted babies suffer as well. In more and more states, lawmakers are holding young men responsible for having sex and getting a girl pregnant. It can cost a father tens of thousands of dollars until the child reaches age eighteen.[12] Along with this financial burden, many carry an emotional burden of guilt and regret. Of vital importance to a Latter-day Saint young man is this direction from the First

Presidency: Any young man who fathers a child or assists in and encourages an abortion is disqualified from serving a mission.[13]

How Can You Avoid the Pain of an Injured Spirit?

Persons who have been immoral lose self-respect and dignity. It may not show on their faces, but inside they experience the pain of an injured spirit. At unexpected times their immoral acts come back to haunt them. It may be something they see or something that is said that keeps it in their memory. Sometimes it becomes a contributing factor to an eating disorder such as bulimia or anorexia. In some critical cases immoral behavior has led to thoughts of suicide. Appropriate repentance (addressed in the last chapter) can help alleviate these problems, and professional counseling may be necessary.

The only absolute protection from these illnesses, burdens, and heartaches when brought on by unchastity is abstaining from any sexual activity until you're married, and then only with your spouse. This once again bears out what the Lord has told his children throughout the ages of time: chastity is your only sure protection.

WHAT ARE THE AFFECTS OF PRE-MARITAL SEX ON MARRIAGE?

Additional reasons proving that it's smart to be morally clean are being discovered by professional marriage counselors, LDS and non LDS alike. As they work with clients with marital problems they find that sexual behavior before marriage takes a heavy—often destructive—toll on marriage relationships. These findings are substantiated by a report from the Family Research Council in Washington, D.C. concluding that

- Couples who engage in sex before marriage are more likely to break up than couples who save sex for marriage.
- Cohabiting unions are much less stable than [unions] that begin as marriages.[14]
- Those who engaged in sex before marriage are more likely to commit adultery than those who had no premarital sexual experience.[15]

Clearly, this is one more piece of evidence that chastity before marriage will greatly benefit the stability and happiness of married partners. When men and women come to the holy altar of matrimony morally clean and pure, their chance of having a lasting, joyful marriage is greatly increased. It creates a trust that is hard to achieve any other way. It shows that their love is on a higher level because patience and sacrifice, two essential elements of a successful marriage, have already been manifested.

True Love Waits

Latter-day Saints are not the only ones who believe in saving sexual intimacy for marriage. When we were in North Carolina to present a fireside to the youth in a stake there, we were looking through the local newspaper that morning. One of the headlines captivated us: *Embracing Chastity*. The article was an account of a gathering of 2000 youth—that's a huge group of kids—from local Protestant churches who had come together in a rally to sign a *True Love Waits* card. The card said: "Believing that true love waits, I make a commitment to God, myself, my family, those I date, my future mate, and my future children to be sexually pure until the day I enter a covenant marriage relationship. Signed ________________."

The article told of a seventeen-year-old girl at the rally who said that dating is easy because she is committed to preserving her virginity. "I've been careful about who I've dated—it gives you an opportunity to know a person for them and not for the physical stuff," she said. "And I'll be able to say to my husband, 'I've been saving this my whole life.'"[16] Another youth told the reporter that adults had given up on them. "Everything—school programs, the media—tell teenagers that adults fully expect them to be promiscuous." He made it clear that they wanted people to know that they weren't being fooled by this and were making a public statement about their commitment to be sexually pure. Some who had not maintained that purity and had repented, expressed gratitude for the ability to now promise to do so. They, and we as Latter-day Saints, are grateful for the loving law of repentance.

How refreshing to hear other youth recognizing that it's smart to stand firm on morality. One of the differences between these youth and you is that you have parents and leaders who *do* expect you to save sex for marriage. We have confidence in you. We don't think you need to sign a card to prove this, although we think it was good that they did. You young people, however, do something far more significant. Every Sunday you partake of the sacrament, and in so doing covenant again with the Lord that you will keep His commandments, which includes being morally clean. We hope you will think of that the next time, and every time, you eat and drink the sacred emblems of the sacrament.

SEX IS SACRED AND BEAUTIFUL

It's important to remember and understand that sex is not evil, but sacred and beautiful when used as God ordained it to be. In its most tender expression in marriage it binds and fortifies the couple's relationship. Through it you will bring forth your precious posterity and fill the measure of your own creation. It is worth every effort to protect and prepare for the divine use of this sacred gift from God.

Remember, to be sexually pure is both a commandment from our loving Father in Heaven and a smart thing to do. We hope you will be wise enough to be *obedient* and *smart*.

Safeguard #2

Choose Well
The Ones You Date

"Cheer up your hearts, and remember that ye are free to act for yourselves—to choose the way of everlasting death or the way of eternal life."
–2 NEPHI 10:23

No one starts out dating by saying, "I'm going to date losers—I just love misery." However, many do date less than desirable people because they don't think seriously about who they're asking out or who they're accepting dates with. Some good-looking girl or guy gives them a little flattery and a smile, and wham! they're hooked into thinking this will be a fun person to go with, without considering what kind of person he or she really is. They are simply enticed and complimented by the attention. Because the person is cute they give or accept the invitation to go on a date.

People don't go around wearing a sign that says "I'm a loser." They do, however, give clues that indicate what kind of person they are. Below are some situations loaded with clues about the person in question. As you read them, seriously ask yourself if this is someone the Savior would want you to date.

GOOD CHOICE/BAD CHOICE

1. You're a girl—you're talking with a group of friends about current movies. Garth, the guy you've been thinking you'd like to go out with, says, "My brother saw this movie last night and said it was awesome." He names the movie, moves closer to you, gives you a nudge and says, "Let's go see it." You're thinking, *He just asked me out! Wow!* Your heart starts beating like a bongo drum. Then you remember the ads for the movie and you know the rating. You're certain it isn't appropriate, so you take a deep breath and say, "I think it's rated R."

Garth says, "No big deal. My brother said there's only a few bad scenes. Let's go, okay?"

2. You're a guy—you've had your eye on Nicole since you were assigned to her study group just a week ago. She's got a smile that makes you want to smile right back. You're attracted to her and wonder what she's really like. A test is coming up and it's a crucial one. Another member of your study group, Gil, has a clever idea for cheating on the test. "No one will know. We've got to pass this one," he says, "so we've got to do whatever it takes." Nicole looks straight at Gil and says, "No way. We study hard, then we pass or fail, but no cheating."

3. You're a girl—you've had your eye on a certain guy for several weeks. He's so cute! You've said "Hi" to him, and he's said "Hi" back, but that's about as far as it's gone. You're walking down the hall at school and when you turn around you see him coming your way. You keep going, hoping he'll say something to you. He walks up behind you, gives you an inappropriate pat on your lower back side and says, "Hey, babe, how about swinging that in my back yard?"

4. You're a guy—you like Karlee. She's cute and popular, and you think you'd like to go out with her. There's only one problem . . . that you know of. She uses what she laughingly calls "colorful" language. The truth is, her conversation is splattered with four-letter words that would make her mother cry.

5. You're a girl—you've been wanting to go out with Kevin, but you don't know him well yet. He's a little shy, but so good looking, and can he play football! Everyone cheers when he's on the field. He's every girl's dream guy; well, anyway, he's the guy *you* dream about. You're in the library and he and his buddies sit next to you. During the quiet conversation you all start talking about the pictures on your driver's licenses. At his buddy's insistence Kevin pulls his wallet out to show him his picture. Since you're sitting next to him, you get a good look, too, but something else catches your eye. Right there in his wallet is a picture of a temple. "Hey, Kev," his buddy says, "What's that?" He replies, "Oh, it's a picture of a special place. I carry it as a reminder."

6. You're a guy—you just moved to a new school. Jason, a student in your math class,

befriends you. He gives you the lowdown on other students. As the two of you walk to your next class, a good looking girl wearing a very tight sweater comes up to you and says, "Hi, you new here?" You answer yes, and, in a flirtatious way, she says, "Well, I think we need to get acquainted." The bell rings and off she goes. You ask Jason about her. He says, "That girl's public property and everybody knows it. She calls herself a 'safe date' and brags about being on the pill."

7. You're a girl—you're at a school party and everyone's dancing and having a great time. You came with a group of your friends and are having a good time with them. A cute guy you've noticed in social studies makes his way to you and asks you for a dance and you happily accept. It's a slow dance and he starts to move in close and you smell it on his breath. He's been drinking!

8. You're a guy—a group of kids are talking about a party coming up at Shara's house that night. You're not sure about going, but are thinking it would be fun to be with everyone, especially Shara. She joins in and says to you, "C'mon.

It's going to be fun. My parents are gone for the weekend and the house will be ours." You know that's a red flag. She sees you hesitating and adds, "You need to lighten up and live a little. We'll have some stuff there to help you out. C'mon."

9. You're a girl—you're hanging out with a bunch of kids in the commons area during lunch, and you've made a point to be near James. Carrie, a girl who has learning disabilities, comes by and says "Hi" to everyone. A couple of the other guys start teasing her in hurtful ways. James looks directly at them and says, "Knock it off!" Then he smiles and says, "Hey, Carrie, you sure do look nice in that jacket. Is it new?"

10. You're a guy—you and several friends including Amy, the girl you've been thinking about asking to the homecoming dance, are riding along in a van on your way to an activity. Someone in the group tells a joke and everyone laughs. Then someone else tells one and it gets contagious. Everyone's laughing and having a great time. Then Kyle takes a turn and tells one that he'd most certainly never tell if the bishop were present. Everyone laughs, except you and

Amy. She's sitting close to Kyle so he notices her lack of response and says, "What's the matter, Amy, too young for a little adult humor?" She politely says, "No. Just sad to hear one of my friends tell a story like that."

11. You're a girl—class is about to start and you're talking with a group of friends, one of which is Jared, the guy you're interested in. His mom runs in from the parking lot and hands him something, and says, "You forgot your book." Jared gives her a little hug, smiles and says, "Thanks, Mom." At that moment you remember your dad saying, "Watch how a guy treats his mother; that's how he'll treat his future wife."

IS IT REALLY "ONLY A DATE?"

There are hundreds of other scenarios we could describe, but you get the idea. It doesn't take a doctorate degree in theology to determine if someone is prime dating material or not. The clues are usually pretty obvious. You may be thinking, "But it's only a date. I'm not going to marry the guy/girl."

Think about this, how many people do you know who married someone they never dated? The truth is, you marry who you date. At no time do you know for sure that a dating relationship won't develop into more than just a friendship. You must be extremely cautious about who you hang out with and who you accept dates from. President Hinckley said, "Choose your friends carefully. It is they who will lead you in one direction or the other . . . never lose sight of [this] fact."[17]

Learn to Say "No" Politely

You are in control of who you choose to be with. You never *have* to accept a date from anyone you don't feel good about. Some people get caught in the trap of thinking it would be rude to say no. There are kind ways to turn someone down, so the fear of appearing rude should never be a reason to accept an invitation with anyone you know you shouldn't be with. Sometimes refusals need to be firm enough that the person won't ask you again.

For example, what could you say to Shara in situation #8? How about, "Thanks, but that's not my kind of party." If she replies with, "Loosen up! You're missing a lot of fun." Just smile and say, "That's the kind of fun I choose to miss. No thanks!" Then change the subject or walk away. This leaves no question about your values. If you give an excuse like, "Sorry, I've already made other plans," she'll be back after you another time.

In situation #7, what could you say to this guy if he, during the dance, asks you to ride home with him? First of all, if you're smart, you'll keep your distance during that slow dance and pray for it to end soon. He'll be well aware that you're keeping him away, and will probably take the hint and won't even ask. But if he does, you might want to refrain from saying, "No way, loser. I don't go with drunks." Just simply say, "No thanks." And if he asks you to dance again, kindly say, "No thanks." There is always a polite way to let someone know you are not interested.

Give the Good Ones a Chance

Sometimes a good guy or girl you're not particularly attracted to may ask you out, and you want to say no. Not every person has to look like a movie star to be a good date. You would be quite surprised to find that many people you may not be attracted to at first, yet who share your values, can be great dates. Give the less popular good guys and girls a chance.

We know of some very happy marriages that began that way. A college student, Michelle, said she was not at all attracted to Ben. She knew he was a good guy—returned missionary and all—but not her type. He persisted and she finally gave in and went with him and some other friends to an amusement park. They had such a good time, she accepted another date. Eight months later they were kneeling at the altar of the temple vowing to love each other for all eternity. Four children later they are even more in love than ever.

You Always Have a Choice

You may live in an area where there are no Latter-day Saints your age to date. What then? Some say, "I have no choice—there's nobody else to date." You always have a choice. That point was driven home when we were speaking at a stake in Rhode Island. We asked the seventeen-year-old son of the family we were staying with, if he had a girlfriend. He said, "No, I have never even had a date, let alone a girlfriend."

This was a good looking, likable guy, so we were surprised and asked how come. He told us it was their family standard that they only date faithful Latter-day Saints. He said, "There are no LDS girls my age, so I don't date. And it isn't easy." His sister had been in the same boat as a teenager and never dated until she went to college where there were other LDS students.

They hang out with friends of other faiths with high standards, but they don't pair off and date. They don't want to risk falling in love with someone they couldn't marry in the temple. We were very impressed with the faith and obedience of these young people. They understood the counsel of President Spencer W. Kimball, who said, "Clearly, right marriage begins with right dating . . . Therefore, this warning comes with great emphasis. Do not take the chance of dating nonmembers, or members who are untrained and faithless. [You] may say, 'Oh, I do not intend to marry this person.' . . . one cannot afford to take a chance on falling in love with someone who may never accept the gospel."[18]

These teens are not alone. We have seen the same dedication in other areas where there are few Latter-day Saints. We are convinced that the Lord will bless these faithful young people in wonderful ways. To the faithful He promises, "Thou shalt observe all these things, and great shall be thy reward" (D&C 42:65). There is no question, the reward will be worth the wait.

Use Moroni's Measuring Rod

Just because a person is LDS and shows up at church meetings does not mean he or she is living the standards of the Church. You must look beyond and know what kind of people they really are. You may be thinking this is judging someone, and you know the Lord said, "Judge not . . ." Don't be misled by this. Of course, we don't judge or condemn people—that's the Lord's job. However, you must make *judgments* when deciding who you associate with.

In the Book of Mormon we're taught how to judge righteously. Moroni said, "I show unto you the way to judge; for every thing which inviteth to do good, and to persuade to believe in Christ . . . ye may know with a perfect knowledge it is of God. But whatsoever thing persuadeth men to do evil, and believe not in Christ, and deny him, and serve not God, then ye may know with a perfect knowledge it is of the devil" (Moroni 7:16-17).

The counsel from the First Presidency of the Church is clear regarding this: "Date only those who have high standards and in whose company you can maintain your standards."[19]

What about you who are not dating age yet? You can look to the not-too-distant future when you will be dating. Fifteen-year-old Richard is a great example. While he was standing in the hall talking to his coach the bell rang for the next class. Soon the hall filled with students. Richard pointed toward a young woman in the crowd and said to the coach, "See that girl right there?" The coach said, "What about her?" Richard said, "That's my future girlfriend." "Oh," said the coach, "and why do you say that?" Richard replied, "She has the best morals of any girl I know." The coach patted him on the back and said, "Good for you." Though

Richard isn't old enough to date, he's making a plan and setting a standard for the kind of girls he will date. It's always smart to plan ahead, then you won't be swept away by just anybody with a pretty face.

WHAT ARE SOME OF SATAN'S TRAPS?

Are people you meet on the Internet in chat stations likely to be good dating material? This kind of relationship can be extremely dangerous. Make it a rule not to chat on line with anyone you don't already know. It's even less safe than walking up to a stranger coming out of a bar and striking up a conversation with him or her. At least you can see what the bar person looks like. On the Internet the person could be a forty-year-old pervert with evil intentions of sexually assaulting you, pretending to be a terrific young guy or girl. Even if the person has no intent to harm you, it is far too easy for people to misrepresent themselves on line. Some people with serious personality defects and a life history that would turn you off in a minute can be very good with words and lead you to believe anything they want. This is just too serious to play with and could lead to disappointment, heartache, or even tragedy, as it has in far too many cases.

You Can Never Count on the Other Person Changing

Sometimes people date those who are less worthy, with the idea that they will bring them up to a higher standard of gospel living. They think, *I'm sure he/she will like me enough to change.* Unfortunately, statistics indicate the opposite will happen. Generally speaking, if you start dating people who lack high standards, you'll end up marrying a person without high standards who quite likely will have pulled you down to his or her level. You must remember that "[the devil] seeketh that all men might be miserable like unto himself" (2 Nephi 2:27). Satan will do all in his power to convince you to follow his way, and when you are with someone who is already following him, you can easily fall. No worthy Latter-day Saint wants that to happen. You must protect yourself by refusing to date those who are not following the Savior and living His standards.

Be careful who you associate with. Jerry was sitting in the library studying when a cute, popular girl came and sat down next to him. He was flattered. She started talking to him about all sorts of things when out of the blue she said, "See that guy over there? I slept with him." Jerry was shocked that she would say such a thing. After gaining his composure he looked at her and said, "Hmmm. And I thought you were a nice girl. I guess I was wrong." She was surprised and said nothing. He got up and left the library. This action clearly defined Jerry's standards, as well as his opinion of the girl's. He protected himself.

Sometimes members *and* nonmembers spiritually lose their way. It doesn't mean they can't make a change. Of course, they can. But you don't know if they will. You can invite them to listen to the missionary discussions. You can invite them to church functions. If they are members you can encourage them to visit their bishop. You can be kind in every way, just as the Savior would want you to be. But you don't date people in that position *until* they have repented and become worthy members of the Church. The risk is just too great.

WHAT ABOUT YOU?

That brings us to that most important question: What kind of person are *you*? Are you someone a faithful Latter-day Saint girl or guy would want to date? Take a careful look at your own values and honestly determine whether or not you are living them. None of us is perfect, but we do need to be on the path that leads there.

When Margie said to her cousin, "I don't know why such scummy guys always ask me out," he was honest and said, "You're attracting these guys by the way you dress and the crude language you use." Margie was a member of the Church who went to some of her meetings on Sunday, but didn't seem to get the message. She said she wanted to date "the good guys," but they just weren't asking her out. Well, no wonder! If you want to date decent people you need to be a decent person yourself. You've got to have *both* feet "on the path."

Questions of Age and Obedience

Part of choosing well when you date is choosing someone who is old enough to date. Our leaders have made it clear that no one should date before the age of sixteen. President Hinckley said, "This rule is not designed to hurt you in any way. It is designed to help you, and it will do so if you will observe it."[20]

One young man who had just turned sixteen was very happy to finally be old enough to take a date to the prom. Problem was, he asked a fifteen-year-old girl to be his date. That's not fair—tempting her to disobey the counsel of the prophet. We need to encourage and help each other be obedient.

Dating can be much more enjoyable when both you and your date are striving to keep the commandments of God. You have less to worry about and more to enjoy together as you seek wholesome activities. It's especially enjoyable when you date in groups. In fact, the counsel from the First Presidency in *For the Strength of Youth* is clear on this subject: "When you begin dating, go in groups or on double dates. Avoid going on frequent dates with the same person." Double dating and dating different people takes the pressure off. That adage "the more the merrier" seems to fit well in the dating scene.

Choose well the people you date and you will be taking a giant step toward protecting your sexual purity and qualifying yourself for all the blessings the Lord has in store for you. He has said, "be thou faithful . . . and I will give thee a crown of life" (Rev. 2:10).

Safeguard #3

Be In Control Of Your Body

"Know ye not that ye are the temple of God . . . If any man defile the temple of God him shall God destroy;"
–1 CORINTHIANS 3:16-17

The next time you look in the mirror notice the wonder of your body. So magnificent is this creation that your Heavenly Father calls it a temple. It's the home where your spirit dwells. Your Father knew you could not experience the joy of eternal life without a body.

Having a body brings many wonderful opportunities, sensations, and pleasures that you would otherwise never experience. It also brings a great responsibility. Because your body is your most precious possession, you must do everything in your power to guard it and control it so you can fulfill the sacred purposes for which it was created.

THE RIGHT TO CHOOSE

Along with receiving your body, you also received the gift of agency—the right to choose. Thus, *you* are the one in control of your body. You are in charge of what you will or won't let happen to it. At any time, you can walk away from a situation that puts the moral purity of your body in jeopardy. The only exception to this is forcible rape. If this has happened to you, please know that you are still morally clean. It was not your choice. If it has happened, talk with your bishop to receive the spiritual support you need to work through such a terrible ordeal. Also, you may need to have professional counseling in order for sexual intimacy to be fulfilling during your future marriage.

What's a Date?

It might be well at this point to define what a date is. Maybe the meaning is obvious to you, but not to some. A fourteen-year-old girl, who had been taught not to date until age sixteen, became pregnant. She said, "But I never had a date." Ah, the naivete of some. Anytime you are paired off with a member of the opposite sex, it's a date.

Choice and Consequences

What happens during that pairing off we define as dating makes all the difference. Just as you have the choice regarding who you will date, you have the choice regarding what you will allow while you're on a date. Your choices in that setting can ruin everything you've dreamed of, or can prepare you for temple worthiness and a happy future.

President Hinckley said, "Date a variety of companions until you are ready to marry. Have a wonderful time, but stay away from familiarity. Keep your hands to yourself. It may not be easy, but it is possible."[21]

SET THE BOUNDARIES

Sometimes difficulty comes from giving messages you may not realize you are giving. For example, you're on a date at a movie and *you like each other.* As you're sitting there your date puts his/her hand on your knee. Your knee is covered so you think it's okay. What if your date moves his/her hand up a few inches higher on your leg? Is that still okay in your mind? And then a few more inches higher. About this time you're certain it's not okay. What's the difference between your knee and higher? When asked that question at our firesides some say, "About ten inches." One young man shouted out, "About ten minutes." Unfortunately, he's probably right.

By allowing your date to put his/her hand on your knee you give the message that your body is available for touching. Small little actions that seem innocent at the time can lead to bigger more disastrous ones. So how do you stop it at the onset and give a clear message to your date? Remember, you like each other. So if the hand ends up on your knee, do you make your statement with a karate chop to the wrist? Ouch! Remember, you like this person. Try this instead. Take your unoccupied hand and gently slip it beneath your date's hand. Your hand becomes the protective barrier between your knee and his/her hand, and clearly says *my body's not available.* Holding your date's hand says, "I like you," while setting a boundary that says, "And you're going no further."

What About Your Own Mason-Dixon Line?

This works in all situations. If your date drapes his hand over your shoulder and it's hanging down in front, what do you do? You take your unoccupied hand and you occupy his hand by holding it. This says, "I like you, and you're going no further." What if he/she puts an arm casually around your back at waist level? Is this okay? That's a relatively safe position; however, sometimes hands wander. Regarding this, here's a boundary to consider.

Remember your Civil War studies and the Mason-Dixon Line? It was a boundary surveyed by two men—Mason and Dixon—that divided the North from the South. For analogy sake here, put on a belt (real or imaginary) at waist level (not hip level) and consider it your Mason-Dixon line. When someone puts an arm around your waist, make sure the hand doesn't go south of the line. If it starts to migrate south, you take your unoccupied hand and hold your date's hand. That clearly says, "I like you, but you're not going any further."

When it comes to the front of the body neither north or south is an option. The front of your body is definitely private territory. The only relatively safe place for your date to touch is the upper center back and only momentarily, and never on bare skin. Speaking of that part of your body, back rubs and massages can be dangerous; they breed familiarity and stir sexual emotions when given by the opposite sex. Save those for your future spouse, unless you're getting physical therapy from a professional.

WHAT ABOUT KISSING?

Because kissing is so enjoyable, it's tempting. Still, it's wise to reserve most kissing for serious courtship and, of course, marriage.

Inappropriate Kissing

There is one kind of kiss that is absolutely *not* appropriate unless you're married. Here's a hint: *Parlez-vous français?* (pronounced parley-voo frahn-say). In case you're not bilingual, we're talking about a French kiss—sometimes called a soul kiss or a deep kiss. This open mouth kissing is much too intimate, and yet it's exactly what is seen in most movies and TV shows. The media does not set the example you should be following. This was emphasized in the booklet *For the Strength of Youth:* "Do not participate in passionate kissing."

President Spencer W. Kimball said, "Kissing has been prostituted and has degenerated to develop and express lust instead of affection, honor, and admiration. To kiss in casual dating is asking for trouble. What do kisses mean when given out like pretzels and robbed of sacredness? What is miscalled the soul kiss is an abomination and stirs passions to the eventual loss of virtue. Even if timely courtship justifies the kiss it should be a clean, decent, sexless one like the kiss between mother and son, or father and daughter."[22]

Hey, we didn't come up with that, a prophet of God did. And who is it that reveals to him what to tell us? It's Jesus Christ, and you need to keep in mind that He will tell you to do *only* that which will lead you to the greatest happiness possible. So when the prophet speaks, listen up!

What Kind of Kisses are Harmless?

The next logical question then, is what kind of kiss is appropriate after you've dated awhile and are becoming serious? It's called a "closed mouth" kiss. Perfectly harmless when it's brief. Get that—brief! It's only when kisses linger that couples get into trouble.

Make Your Own Kissing Plan

You are in control of who receives a kiss from you as well as the length of that kiss. Have you made a plan about who, when, and how long?

A few years ago we were sitting in the Marriott Center at Brigham Young University listening to General Authorities speak to the student members of stakes in that region. President James E. Faust (then Elder Faust) and his wife were addressing the congregation. She spoke first, then before she had a chance to sit down, he walked up, put his arm around her and said, "Would you like to know when I first kissed her?" All heads nodded yes, probably hoping he wasn't going to say "over the altar." He said, "It was when I asked her to marry me. I had decided to wait until that moment, and it was a right decision for me." Then he smiled that playful smile of his and said, "And I've been making up for it ever since." He encouraged the students there to make decisions that would be right for them, decisions that would lead them to a temple marriage. What are your decisions? We urge you to make a kissing plan right now.

NECKING AND PETTING

We cannot express enough how important it is to guard your body, to be alert and aware of the dangers and sorrows that happen when a person allows another to handle his or her body. President Spencer W. Kimball was very explicit in warning us about these dangers. He said, "Among the most common sexual sins our young people commit are necking and petting. Not only do these improper relations often lead to fornication, pregnancy, and abortions—all ugly sins—but in and of themselves they are pernicious evils, and it is often difficult for youth to distinguish where one ends and another begins. They awaken lust and stir evil thoughts and [sexual] desires.

It Happened Then, Too

"[The apostle] Paul wrote as if to modern young people who deceive themselves that their necking and petting are but expressions of love: 'Wherefore God also gave them up to uncleanness through the lusts of their own hearts, to dishonour their own bodies between themselves' (Romans 1:24). How could the evils of petting be more completely described?"[23]

Every Person Has a Breaking Point

You may be thinking, "but I would never let it go *that* far." Most good Latter-day Saints don't intend to get caught in this trap. So how does it happen to such good people? President Kimball gave the answer: "The devil knows how to destroy [you]. He may not be able to tempt a person to . . . commit [sexual sins] immediately, but he knows that if he can get a boy and a girl to sit in the car late enough after the dance, or to park long enough in the dark at the end of the lane, the best boy and the best girl will finally succumb and fall. He knows that all have a limit to their resistance."[24]

Sure-Fire Passion Stoppers

If you find yourself in a position where a guy starts to get too chummy and you can't seem to get him away from you, here's something that will work. Grab your stomach and give a big moan and say, "On, no. I've got diarrhea! I've got to get to a toilet quick." Or try this one: Put your hand over your mouth and say, "I'm about to lose my dinner. I've got to get to a bathroom right now." If you need to be convincing then make yourself sound like "it" is on the way up. Either of these actions will stop any guy cold. All sexual desire will be doused like water dumped on a flame and he's going to get you home fast. Don't stop the act until you're safely inside. This is one of the few scenarios where premeditated deception could be considered virtuous and praiseworthy. A girl's gotta do what a girl's gotta do to protect her sexual purity—and so does a guy.

Recognizing the Steps

When my husband was a bishop a young woman came into his office to confess her immorality. She was heartbroken. This was a young woman who had planned all her life for a temple marriage. She went away to college and met a wonderful young man who had the same goals she did. Before she knew it, the unthinkable had happened. Through her tears she said, "I don't know how it happened, Bishop. I never meant to do it."

He was deeply touched by her desire to repent and by the remorse she felt. To help awaken in her a knowledge of how it happened, he had her trace her steps with her boyfriend to discover how it *did* happen. She needed to be fully aware so that it would never be repeated. In tracing these steps they came up with a plan of action that would safeguard against that ever happening again.

First, here are the steps that led—one by one—to her downfall:

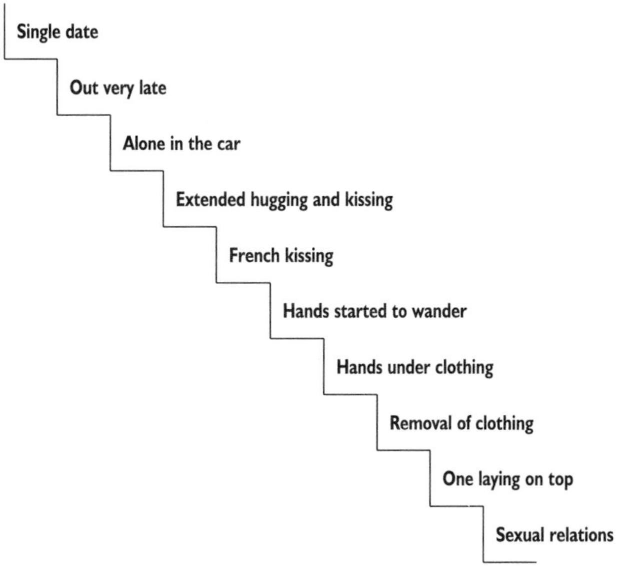

Then came the sorrow and shame that inevitably come to those who break this sacred commandment.

Her bishop helped her understand that these steps led her down and away from moral purity and that there are steps she could take to replace them that would lead up and keep her on the road to temple worthiness. The following are the steps the bishop helped her come up with:

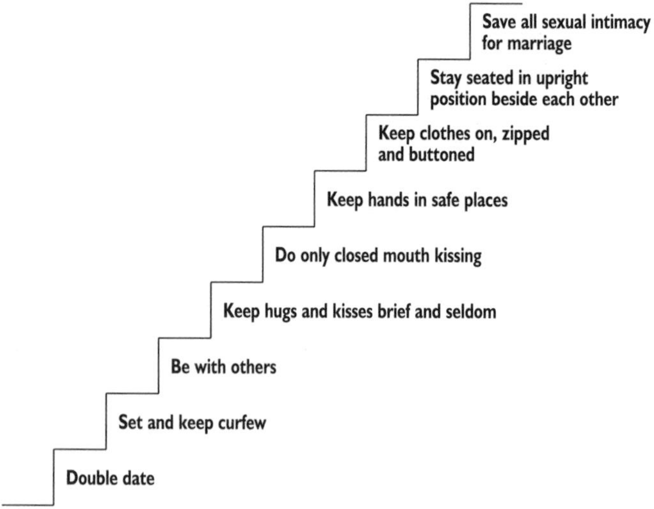
Save all sexual intimacy for marriage
Stay seated in upright position beside each other
Keep clothes on, zipped and buttoned
Keep hands in safe places
Do only closed mouth kissing
Keep hugs and kisses brief and seldom
Be with others
Set and keep curfew
Double date

These are the same steps that will keep you temple worthy if you have never lost your virtue. These actions will protect you from Satan's power. Reread them, memorize them, and live them.

Also, protect yourself by following these additional safeguards when you're dating.

- Avoid sexual talk and innuendoes.
- Enjoy uplifting conversations with each other—share knowledge and ideas.
- Stay awake—don't fall asleep near your date.
- Don't take trips with a person you're dating.
- Carry a cell phone, if you have one, and ask your parents to call you if you're late.
- Limit the time you spend with each other, *including when you're engaged to be married.*

There's a popular saying that applies here: Don't give up what you want most for what you want now. By living these safeguards you will one day find yourself in your bishop's office, not in deep remorse to confess sins of immorality, but to look him in the eyes with a clear conscience and a feeling of gratitude as he interviews you for your temple recommend.

SAFEGUARD YOUR SELF-RESPECT

President Kimball made another statement that has been validated many times: "Our young people should know that their partners in sin will not love or respect them if they have freedom in fondling their bodies."[25] If you allow your date to handle your body, no matter how much in love you profess to be, the day will likely come when you will be cast aside by that person. Even though they never get around to showing this part in immoral movies, illicit sexual behavior kills love. Alma understood this truth when he said, 'See that ye bridle all your passions that ye may be filled with love'" (Alma 38:12).

Time and time again we have seen people in real life abandoned by their "lover" after having sexual relations. They lose respect for each other and one or both no longer wants to be in the relationship. If people would just bridle their passions, their boyfriend or girlfriend would have greater respect and deeper love for them.

Nephi, like our latter-day leaders, was so sad at the immorality of his people that he cried out to them, "Yea, how could you have given way to the enticing of him who is seeking to hurl away your souls down to everlasting misery and endless wo?" (Helaman 7:16). You must be smart enough to understand the subtle ways that Satan works to snare you in his awful trap.

Why the Word of Wisdom Is So Wise

Another way he works to cause you to lose your virtue is through violation of the Word of Wisdom. The Lord gave you this commandment to protect you (D&C 89). When you *don't* drink alcoholic beverages or partake of illicit drugs, you are able to stay in control of your body. Taking these harmful substances is, plainly and simply, giving your body over to the adversary, whose whole desire is to hurt you. No sensible person would do that. A campus police officer said, "Partaking of alcohol and drugs are very destructive because they open the door to all the other sins."

Treat Your Body As the Temple It Is

Satan uses every available method to weaken your resolve to be morally clean. In the booklet *For the Strength of Youth*, under the Sexual Purity section, this instruction was also given: "Do not arouse [sexual] emotions in your own body." To touch yourself in private places to cause sexual pleasure is wrong. It becomes addictive and fills your mind with inappropriate thoughts. President Kimball said, "Prophets anciently and today condemn masturbation. It induces feelings of guilt and shame. It is detrimental to spirituality. It indicates slavery to the flesh, not . . . mastery of it."[26] This action often leads to more serious moral transgressions and should not be done.

You are the one who will make the choices regarding your body. Through the inspiration of the Holy Ghost you will know what you should and should not be doing to it. Everyone has choices to make, and because you know the truth, they will be clear to you. President Thomas S. Monson gave a simple, easy to remember formula to measure these choices. He said, "You can't be right by doing wrong and you can't be wrong by doing right."[27]

In all things regarding your moral purity, remember that your body is a temple and must be controlled by you. Treat it with respect, much as you would the holy temple where you will one day make sacred covenants and be married for time and all eternity to your own true love.

Safeguard #4

Fill Your Mind With Good Things

"Let virtue garnish thy thoughts unceasingly."
–D&C 121:45

Pretend that you are invited to an elegant buffet dinner. Knowing it will be overflowing with the most exquisite cuts of meat and all your favorite fruits, vegetables, and desserts prepared to perfection, you can hardly wait to go. When you enter the room, you look at the display from a distance and are captivated by the beauty of the setting. Music fills the air, silver candelabras with glowing candles and exotic flowers of every variety are artistically placed among the crystal serving dishes that are loaded with food fit for a king. You are hungry and lick your lips in anticipation. You take your plate and move closer to begin filling it with the delicacies you came to enjoy. As you look closely at the food, you are stunned! Intermingled with the good food you long to partake of, you see pieces of rotten meat and other food items that are covered with mold and crawling with maggots. Will you stay and try to pick out the items of food you like, hoping they won't be infected? Or will you leave as quickly as you can, to get away from any possibility of being contaminated?

WALK AWAY

This story could be likened to an experience told to us by a young Latter-day Saint named Matt. He was invited by a group of his friends to go to a movie that had just been released. He didn't know much about the movie, but the rating seemed okay and he had heard it was good. As he and his buddies were sitting in the theater watching it, a scene came on that was shocking. It was blatantly immoral and he knew he shouldn't be watching it. He knew what to do. He got up and was about to walk out when one of his friends asked, "Hey, where ya going?" Matt whispered, "I'll be in the lobby." He found a seat where he could wait for his friends until the movie was over.

To Matt's surprise, in just a few minutes one of his friends came out and joined him. The friend said, "Pretty gross, huh?"

"Yea, it is," Matt replied.

A few minutes later another friend came out. Before long they were all out and left the theater. Matt's decision to protect himself from scenes of immorality helped his friends have the courage to also make that choice.

You Can't Throw Up "a Few Bad Scenes"

Contrast this with the young man in chapter two whose comment about an R rated movie was, "No big deal . . . there's only a few bad scenes." Frankly, it's a very big deal. Obviously, you cannot partake of the good in this kind of a movie without also being affected by the bad. As with the food, you cannot help but become contaminated by it.

The difference is that with contaminated food you can throw up and purge it from your body, take antibiotics to kill the infection it may cause, and in most cases be rid of it. Not so with visual images. Our brains keep everything inside. No medicine has yet been developed to cleanse the brain of unwanted images. The "few bad scenes" will linger in your mind even though you try not to remember them. They are there and they will influence the way you think and act.

SATAN IS A DIRTY FIGHTER

How do good people get tricked into going to events that will be destructive to their spirits? It happens through the clever devices of Satan. He decorates his evil events with much the same exuberance and extravagance that the buffet feast had. He employs top-of-the-line talent, decks them out in bizarre and immodest clothing to attract attention, and then spends millions of dollars to convince people that they wouldn't want to miss this for the world. He even persuades certain famous, "respected" people to praise the event and the performers, and to encourage others to attend it.

It's a very cunning plan he uses to ensnare the innocent. He wants nothing more than to capture good-living people like you, deaden your sense of right, and ruin your life. His whole purpose is to drag you down to his depth of misery. We remind you again of the truth Nephi taught when he said, "[The devil] seeketh that all men might be miserable like unto himself" (2 Nephi 2:27). Elder M. Russell Ballard said, "The devil is a dirty fighter, and we must be aware of his tactics."[28]

Win With Vigilance and Foreknowledge

To protect yourself you must be on guard at all times. The apostle Peter understood Satan's plan and strongly warned us to "Be sober, be vigilant; because your adversary the devil, as a roaring lion, walketh about, seeking whom he may devour" (1 Peter 5:8). To more fully understand this scripture let's explore the meanings of the words "sober" and "vigilant." Everyone knows that "sober" means "not drunk," but its other meanings bring even more clarity to Peter's warning. It also means "to be serious; showing mental and emotional balance." "Vigilant" means "staying watchful and alert to danger and trouble."[29] So his instruction to us is that we must be seriously aware, mentally and emotionally, of Satan's strategies, and watchful so that we are not lured into his traps. How do we do this? Consider the following analogy.

Players on a ball team always have a game plan. They know their plays well and practice them continually so they will be prepared to meet the opposing teams. They also watch the other teams play so they will know *their* game plans. When they know how the other team plays, it allows them to be more effective in their defense and puts them in a better position to win the game. To take this a step further, can you imagine what an advantage it would be in a war if you knew the enemy's plan? You would win the war.

Fortunately for us we have living prophets who know the enemy's plan and are familiar with his strategies. We remind you once again of President Hinckley's warning, "The adversary of truth would like to injure you, would like to destroy your faith, would like to lead you down paths that are beguiling and interesting, but deadly."[30]

Our leaders have warned us that one of Satan's most important goals is to cause Latter-day Saints to lose their moral purity. He knows if he can get you to think it's all right to use your sexuality inappropriately, he can win. That's why you must be in control of your own mind and what goes into it at all times.

THE ADVERSARY'S WEAPONS

Satan has many weapons to weaken that control. Here are four of them:

1. All forms of entertainment and the media can be used by Satan for his purposes.

President Benson said, "Don't see R-rated movies or vulgar videos or participate in any entertainment that is immoral, suggestive, or pornographic."[31] He said that before there was a PG-13 rating. Most movies today with the PG-13 rating probably would have been rated R then. In a magazine article titled *The Enemy Among Us,* Keith Merrill, an LDS Academy-award winning director, wrote: "It is of particular interest to me that the Church has elected to abandon the MPAA rating system as a reliable guideline for youth. . . . This is not to be interpreted that the

Church approves of R-rated movies or any other inappropriate movies. It is simply a recognition that there is increasingly great risk in tying ourselves to any rating system. The pamphlet [*For the Strength of Youth*] says clearly, 'Do not attend, view, or participate in entertainment that is vulgar, immoral, violent, or pornographic in any way.' "[32] That's very clear.

We have already discussed how cleverly Satan uses the media to try to persuade you to follow his ways. He puts his brightest stars in the spotlight with the hope that you will not resist the temptation to go see them in movies, videos, and concerts that promote immorality. This is the moment when you must be on guard. You know the enemy's plan—don't fall for it. You have the counsel of the prophets—follow it.

Some say, "Oh, it won't have any power over me. My testimony is strong." That's like jumping into a lake of red hot lava, saying "I'll be fine. I've got my cell phone with me." Your testimony is not going to protect you when you go places you know you shouldn't go. If your testimony is strong, you will listen to the whisperings of the Spirit, and you won't go.

Remember that good decisions build trust. One evening a teenage brother and sister and a couple of their friends came into the family room where their father sat reading. They said, "Hey, Dad. There's a new program on TV tonight and we want to watch it. Okay?" He said, "Sure, as long as you promise me that you'll shut it off if any of the actors break any of the Lord's commandments." They agreed, and he went into the other room to read. A few minutes later they were all in the kitchen raiding the fridge. Dad said, "I thought you were watching that new show." His son replied, "We were, but ten minutes into the show they started breaking the commandments. We shut it off. That was the deal." This actually happened, and these kids had one proud dad. He knew he could trust them.

You have a Father in Heaven who has made that same kind of deal with you. He wants you to have fun and enjoy good movies. There is good, wholesome entertainment out there and He wants you to be able to enjoy it, but to be smart enough to shut off the TV or leave the theater if the actors are breaking His commandments. He trusts you to do it. That's the deal.

2. Pornography in books, magazines, and the Internet has become a powerful weapon in Satan's arsenal.

President Hinckley gave a clear warning: "Pornography, with its sleazy filth, sweeps over the earth like a horrible, engulfing tide. It is poison. Do not watch it or read it. It will destroy you if you do."[33] At a BYU devotional he told the students to "Recognize it for what it is—a vicious brew of slime and sleaze, the partaking of which only leads to misery, degradation, and regret."[34] At a General Conference priesthood session, he told of a man who became addicted to this evil and felt great despair from it. In a letter to the prophet he wrote, "I think it is ironic that those who support the business of pornography say that it is a matter of freedom of expression. I have no freedom. I have lost my free agency because I have been unable to overcome this. It is a trap for me, and I can't seem to get out of it. Please, please, please, plead with the brethren of the Church to not only avoid but eliminate the sources of pornographic material in their lives."[35]

Mark Kastleman, author of the book *The Drug of the New Millennium: Internet Pornography,* told us about a twelve-year-old boy he interviewed. The boy had accidentally clicked on a porn site that pulled him into one site after another during a period of about two weeks. He found that his mind could think of almost nothing else. The images stayed with a power that kept pulling him into more and more pornography sites. He began failing at school. He began to lose interest in his friends. His relationship with his family was suffering. At one point he felt so terrible and so possessed by the horrible habit he was beginning to fall into, that he made a decision. This young man took control of the situation and decided that, no matter how difficult, he would never look at pornography sites again. He said, "Pornography makes you stupid." He quit cold turkey and kept his promise to himself. He got his life back and said he never wants anything like that to happen to him again.

If anyone is trapped into this terrible addiction of pornography, there is a way out. Those who have been involved longer may not be able to conquer this destructive habit as quickly as this young man did, but it can be done. Elder Jeffrey R. Holland said, "In the moral realm the only real control you have is self control."[36] For those struggling to overcome the problem of pornography we suggest the following method. Many therapists and bishops have helped others succeed with these simple and effective steps.

• Pray morning and night in *very specific words* asking the Lord to help you stop and to be able to stay away from any kind of pornography. Pray anytime, day or night, when tempting thoughts come into your mind.

• Go to your bishop and talk to him about your problem. He will be there as a representative of the Savior with a loving heart, ready to help you. You may want to ask him for a priesthood blessing to help you have the strength to completely repent and resist the temptation.

• Talk to your parents or other trustworthy family members about your problem. They will be your everyday sustaining influence. Even if they are not members of the Church, they probably understand the destructive power of pornography and will help you. You will most likely find them to be compassionate and honored that you are seeking their help.

• Keep track of and celebrate your successes. To do this, take a small calendar with a blank box at each date, and keep it in a private place. Keep a marking pen or pencil of your favorite color near it. When you have gone twenty-four hours without viewing any pornography, mark a dot in the box.

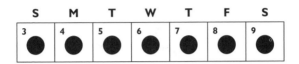

S	M	T	W	T	F	S
3 ●	4 ●	5 ●	6 ●	7 ●	8 ●	9 ●

Continue doing this each day. When you have gone seven days, privately celebrate your success by buying yourself a small candy bar or other special treat. When you've gone two weeks, celebrate with a larger treat. Same for the third week. At the end of a month of successes buy yourself a new shirt, a CD you've been wanting, or something else you'd really like. Each time you celebrate, you acknowledge to yourself that you're succeeding at overcoming this problem.

Why Is It Important to Focus on the Days You Succeed?

Here's a caution: often when someone is trying to overcome this evil habit and they slip once, they get discouraged and think they're a failure and can't overcome it. Yes, you can—just change your thinking. Instead of getting discouraged, look at all the times you did succeed and start again. Maybe you did great thirteen out of fourteen days. Pat yourself on the back for the thirteen days, which is so much better than you were doing before you started this program. Then keep going, marking every successful day. If you were a basketball player and hit thirteen out of fourteen shots, you'd be praised to the hilt by coaches and teammates. Close your eyes and imagine that the Lord is praising you for your successful days. Pray with all your might and continue marking your calendar. You will soon be able to look back and see a calendar full of successful days, with no slips. That's your goal.

Two brothers who came to a therapist for help with this problem tried this method. One was diligent and kept on with the calendar, even when he slipped a few times. Before long, he had completely overcome the problem and is now serving a mission. His brother, on the other hand, sadly gave up and stopped trying. His life has gone in a different direction, filled with sorrow and loss of self-respect.

Stick with this method and you will begin to realize the success you are praying for.

Even More Protection Ideas

Here are some additional tips that will help you overcome this addictive behavior.

• Keep a Book of Mormon or some other good book or church magazine on a nightstand near your bed. If a pornographic image comes into your mind or you have the urge to look at such material, take the book in both of your hands, turn on the light and read a few verses from it. Keep reading until the urge leaves you and you instead have these good things to ponder in your mind. Fill your room with good wholesome books, magazines, music, and posters that you can turn to for protection from the power of evil. Also you may need to do the following.

• Leave your room and go to where other family members are. If no one is home, go outside and take a walk where people are.

• If the Internet is your problem, move your computer out of your room into the family room or more public place, facing out, not toward the wall. Protect yourself every way you possibly can.

• Sometimes people get into pornographic sites without meaning to at all. You have the guidance of the Holy Ghost with you and you will know if, for instance, an unsolicited e-mail will be pornographic or not. There are clues and you're not stupid. Don't be curious enough to fall into Satan's trap. If you accidentally click on a porn site, immediately delete it. Sadly, some of these sites are set up to keep you locked into them and sometimes a click to delete will move you to another awful picture. If this happens, pull the plug on your computer. Sometimes this is the only way out. It won't hurt your computer, but it will hurt you terribly if you stay on line trying other ways to get out. The cleverness of Satan must be acknowledged and prepared for. Just pull the plug.

• Get an Internet filter on your computer. They are not expensive and will help screen out unwanted e-mail and Web sites that contain harmful material. Talk with your parents about this kind of protection for you and your family.

You and Your Family Are Worth Whatever Effort It Takes

When it comes to pornography every precaution must be taken. This evil can have a devastating affect on your life now *and* your future marriage relationship. In a General Conference priesthood session President Hinckley said, "The girl you marry is worthy of a husband whose life has not been tainted by this ugly and corrosive material."[37] And, of course, that applies to girls as well. Sometimes young women get caught up in reading titillating novels and glitzy magazines that describe inappropriate sexual behavior. This is another form of pornography and must be avoided as fervently as any other pornographic material.

3. The adversary can use music as a weapon.

Inappropriate music can drive away the Spirit. Some people don't realize the power music has to influence their thinking. President Benson said, "Listen to uplifting music both popular and classical, that builds the spirit. Learn some favorite hymns . . . Attend dances where the music and the lighting and the dance movements are conducive to the Spirit."[38]

One young man told his parents that he was living righteously and his music, which taught immorality among other sins, was not hurting him.

His parents tried to convince him to stop listening to this hard music, but he would not heed their counsel. He went on a mission and after a few months he went to his mission president, begging for some help. He said that no matter how hard he tried he could not get the terrible lyrics of the music out of his head. He said, "I can't feel the Spirit and I can't concentrate on my mission. I want to be a good missionary. Please help me get rid of the terrible lyrics and music in my head." After much fasting, prayer, and a priesthood blessing he finally found relief. Inappropriate music will, one way or another, eventually take a terrible toll on you.

Elder William R. Bradford said, "Listen to and sing the music of heaven. Reject the vulgar and base sounds and beats of Satan's music. He would like to gain your favor with his sensual and carnal rhythms and thereby lead you down to hell."[39] In an effort to combat the influence of Satan's music many musicians in the Church have written and performed inspiring music. We have come to love and appreciate the works of many of these artists. Janice Kapp Perry and I have also written many songs with that same hope. We've received numerous comments and letters from young people expressing gratitude for music that has helped them stay strong. A young woman from Ohio said, "Having these words and melodies in my mind has helped me remember who I am and gives me the courage to live morally clean."

There are many gifted composers and musicians, LDS and non-LDS, who are creating good, uplifting music that young people are enjoying. Start collecting your own favorites, remembering that music has the power to lift you up and help you reach your eternal goals. Surround yourself with good music.

4. Alcohol and illegal drugs are powerful weapons in Satan's arsenal.

If you take these into your body you lose control of not only your body, but your mind. These substances can alter your thinking. Things you would never do if you had not taken them, appear to be okay. Your brain is desensitized. To stay in control of your ability to think wisely and protect yourself, never partake of any of these.

President Hinckley vigorously warned the members of the Church about these substances. He said, "Do not become involved in illegal drugs. Do not touch them. Never experiment with them. I plead with you, to shun them as you would poison."[40] He knows that people who use these substances will lose control of their ability to think clearly and make wise choices. They will no longer be able to feel the Spirit guiding them. The drugs will take control.

PROTECT YOURSELF

Sometimes sexual thoughts will come into your mind, as if from nowhere. Should this happen, don't condemn yourself. This is normal. However, what you do about it is significantly important. Do not entertain these thoughts. Replace them with good thoughts by singing a hymn or a favorite uplifting song. If you're alone sing it out loud; if others are around sing it silently in your mind. Even just saying the words will do the trick. Elder Boyd K. Packer suggested that members memorize the words of a favorite hymn to use on just such occasions.

The M&Ms That Strengthen and Protect

Memorizing uplifting material maximizes your ability to ward off Satan's advances. That's why we call this strategy M&Ms—*Memorize and Maximize* your power to ward off Satan. When our children were teens we did scripture memorizing with them. They weren't what you would call "eager beavers," but we persisted. And they responded, since it was a prerequisite to breakfast, and they liked eating. We hope this practice has served them well—we know it has helped us when we've needed a scripture to turn to. We encourage you, too, to memorize a few scriptures. One of our sons said, "Let's memorize the one that says, 'Jesus wept.' It won't take so long." That's not a bad idea. Go ahead and memorize that one. When you repeat it, just imagine the reality of it. Picture Jesus weeping in the Garden of Gethsemane as He suffered for your sins. Picture Him looking down on you now and do all in your power to make sure that any tears He sheds over you will be tears of happiness because of how hard you are trying to do what is right. Yes, "Jesus wept" is a good one to memorize and repeat when you need a worthy thought.

Also memorize other favorite scriptures. They will remind you of how much the Lord loves you and wants you to be happy.

President Thomas S. Monson is a great example of one who memorizes poetry and scriptures. It's amazing how many poems and scriptures he has on the tip of his tongue. If you memorize an inspiring poem or scripture, when you need a good thought it will be right there in your mind.

Your Mind Deserves the Very Finest Food

President David O. McKay said, "Resist the devil and he will flee from you. Court him and you shall soon have shackles, not on your wrists but on your soul."[41] To help in your determination to resist him, take every opportunity to fill your mind with the good things in life. Recognize what a beautiful world we have and how filled with opportunities for doing good it is. Develop your talents and you will always have something worthwhile and enjoyable to do when you have free time. Share these talents with others and bring a light into their lives. Read good books that show how other good men and women have lived. Read novels that motivate you to accomplish goodness in your own life. Listen to music that lifts your spirit. Attend concerts that heighten your awareness of the beauty the Lord has created for us.

As you do these things your mind will then overflow with good thoughts that will help you maintain your moral purity. In essence, as the thirteenth Article of Faith states, "If there is anything virtuous, lovely, or of good report or praiseworthy . . . seek after these things."

Safeguard #5

Watch What You Wear

"Shine as lights in the world."
–PHILIPPIANS 2:15

The spotlight is on, and down the ramp walks a lovely young woman modeling the latest fashion in formal wear. The audience is in awe. Her gown is exquisitely fashioned in a shimmering satin of silvery blue. Her shoulders are covered with delicately draped inset sleeves. The figure-flattering A-line skirt gently swirls to her ankles. She wears the first of an array of beautiful modestly-styled gowns being modeled by other lovely young women for this prestigious crowd. Who are they? They are royalty—sons and daughters of God who are taking a stand. They are a ward of youth, leaders, and parents who will no longer be controlled by what the world considers the "in" styles. They've had it! And they're coming forth "as lights in the world."

We Are On Earth to Act, Not to Be Acted Upon

This is not a contrived situation. It's happening in wards and stakes all over. We first heard of it when two young women from a ward near Kansas City took the initiative to do something when they went looking for prom dresses in Nordstrom's department store. There wasn't even one dress on the racks that would be appropriate for a Latter-day Saint girl to wear. They politely, yet resolutely, took their complaint to the management, who asked them to put on a fashion show exhibiting the style of dresses they preferred.

The girls, with the help of mothers and young women leaders, worked for four months to prepare the presentation for the Nordstrom executives. The word spread via church and Internet and the store received "more than 2,500 letters and e-mails . . . from young women around the world who said they'd be interested in more modest fashions."[42] The executives began to realize that these girls were only a small part of a very large number of young women throughout the world who feel the same way. The buyer promised that more modest clothing would be available in the future. Since then other wards and stakes have sponsored their own modesty fashion shows and given ideas on how to make clothing more in line with what the Lord would want Latter-day Saint women to wear.

What Can You Do?

Speaking at a General Young Women's Conference, President Faust gave another suggestion: "You young ladies may have a hard time buying a modest prom dress. May I suggest that you make your own? You may need some help, but plenty of help is available."[43] He's right, there *is* plenty of help available. If your mother or other family member can't help you, ask your Young Women leader or a member of the Relief Society presidency. They all know women who can sew and would be delighted to help a young woman have a beautiful, modest prom dress.

A mother in Las Vegas made her daughter a modest dress for the prom. A few days after the prom when she showed her prom pictures to her friends who are not members of our Church, they exclaimed, "We love your dress; you look like Cinderella! Where can we get a dress just like that?"[44] Now her mother is in a successful business of making modest prom and bridesmaid dresses for others.

Parents Who Really Care

Other ways parents can come to the rescue are illustrated in an experience I had as a youth. It was my dream to go to the prom, and at last I was sixteen and eligible—but no one was asking me. Finally, with only a week to go, I got a date! He was not my dream guy, but he was nice, and I was very happy. I could hardly wait to tell my mother the good news.

I lived on a farm in Oregon and rode the school bus home every day. When I arrived at my stop on this day I jumped off and ran the half mile home. I dashed into the house yelling, "Mom, I got a date!" My mother was excited, too, and I enjoyed every minute telling her all about it. Then I realized I had a serious problem—I didn't have a thing to wear. Nor did I have the money to buy a new dress. The only job I had was helping out at home, which was a necessity because I belonged to a large family of mostly boys who helped on the farm. I had no extra money stashed under my mattress for emergencies like this.

My mom had lots of talents—cooking, cleaning, even singing with the ward choir—but she couldn't sew. Oh, she could hem dish towels and a few things like that, but you don't wear dish towels to the prom. I was worried. My mother understood and said, "I'll talk to Dad tonight and we'll see if we can buy you a formal for the prom." This sounded good, but I had asked my dad for things before and he had replied, "I wish we could, honey, but there just isn't enough money." I had every reason to be worried.

After the discussion that evening my parents came to me, and Dad said, "This is really important to you, isn't it?" With great sincerity I replied,

"Daddy, for this purpose I was born." He understood, and said I could buy a formal for the dance. I was so happy and threw my arms around his neck and thanked him profusely. My mother said, "I'll pick you up after school tomorrow and we'll go shopping."

The next day Mom was there right on time and the shopping began. Now this was during the mid 1950s and the style for formals then was strapless. When my mother and I entered the dress shop, all we could see were strapless evening gowns. Not even anything ugly that covered the shoulders. All strapless. You need to understand that my parents had taught me well the words of the current prophet, President David O. McKay. He had made it clear that women should dress modestly. Sound familiar? Some things never change—modesty is always in style with the Lord. I knew these formals were not modest. So we went to another shop, and found the same thing—every dress hanging on the racks was strapless. I thought, *How can they hang there?* Think about it.

On we went to the next shop. About this time I began to realize that if there was nothing else in the stores, all the girls would be wearing strapless evening gowns at the prom. Suddenly, I wanted to be "in." When we entered the next shop I saw it hanging there—a beautiful formal, in *my* color! Oh, it was strapless all right, but it was beautiful. I said, "Mom, can I try it on? I know I can't get it, but could I just try it on and see if I look good in this color?" My mother agreed.

In the dressing room I put it on and looked into the mirror. It was stunning. I thought, *I have to have this dress.* So I walked out for my mother to see and said, "Mom, we've looked everywhere and there just isn't anything, so we're forced into this purchase." My mother said, "No, we're not. But it is your color and it does come up nice and high, so I've got an idea. We'll get some material to match it and I'll make a little covering for your shoulders." I was somewhat disappointed that I wouldn't be wearing it strapless, but without letting that disappointment show, I agreed. We went home with my dream dress and the material.

The next day before my mother had any chance to work on the covering for my shoulders, the phone rang. It was my brother calling all the way from Provo, Utah where he and his wife were attending BYU. The very first grandchild in the family had just been born. My mother was so excited and her help was badly needed. She was on a bus to Provo in a matter of hours, and forgot all about making the covering for my formal.

The night of the prom arrived and my mother was still gone. Everything was going just as I had dreamed; I even had a good hair day. When I was all ready I looked into the mirror and thought, *tonight is the night I live!* Fifteen minutes before my date was to arrive I walked out into the living room. And there was my father! He took one look at me and said, "Where did you get *that* dress?"

I said, "Mother bought it for me." He said, "Mother would never buy that dress without a plan. Now you tell me the plan." I said, "Oh, Daddy, there was a plan. We bought some material and Mother was going to make a covering for my shoulders and she didn't have time, and I don't know how to. So, well, Daddy, I'm just sick about it but I have to go this way." Without any preaching, my wise father said, "Where's the material? Get it for me quickly, and bring a needle and thread and the scissors." I knew it was smart to obey my father, but was feeling panicky because I had never seen him sew anything but seeds.

He took the material, laid it on the table and folded it over several times until it was a strip about eight inches wide. Then he took one end of the strip and carefully stitched it to one side of the top of my dress—using little tiny stitches. Not the kind that can be pulled, and zip, they're gone. No, they were there for the night. Then he brought the strip of material around the back of my shoulders, clipped off the excess and carefully stitched it to the other side in front. And I was modest. As he did it, I thought, *tonight is the night I die!*

Then he stood back, looked at me and said, "You look beautiful." I ran into my room to look in the mirror, and to my surprise it didn't look bad at all. The ruffles on the dress hid the stitches and it looked like it belonged. Not what I had wanted, but not bad. Just then the doorbell rang and off I went to the prom with my date.

That night as I danced around amidst all those bare shoulders, something happened. No one else knew it happened because it happened inside of me. I began to realize how much my parents loved me. Even though it wasn't easy, they had done all in their power to help me obey the prophet. Since then I have come to realize that you can't get greater love than that, because it is through this obedience that you can enjoy the greatest happiness possible.

Probably nothing bad would have happened to me that night, but here's what might have happened, and if it had it would have been one of the saddest things of all. I might have really enjoyed being "of the world" and would have done more and more things contrary to the teachings of the prophets and been led carefully away by Satan. Then I would never have been married in the temple to my wonderful husband. That would have been a real tragedy.

MODESTY IS NOT ONLY ABOUT FORMALS

Formals are not the only concern when it comes to modesty. Many popular everyday fashions reveal parts of the body that should be covered. In the booklet *For the Strength of Youth,* it says, "Immodest clothing includes short shorts and skirts, tight clothing, shirts that do not cover the stomach, and other revealing attire. Young women should wear clothing that covers the shoulder and avoid clothing that is low-cut in the front or the back or revealing in any other manner."

What Is the "Modesty Test?"

Whenever you buy a piece of clothing you need to give it the "modesty test." Always try it on at the store and look at yourself in the mirror. Lean over and look at your image to see if the cut is too low, revealing private parts of your body. Then stand up and raise your arms to see if it will expose your mid section. Sometimes it appears to be okay until you lean over or raise your arms. If it's a skirt, turn around and lean over again, looking back into the mirror to see what others will see when you bend over. Be aware of slits in skirts. Some are extreme. Some seem fine when you're standing, but reveal far too much when you sit or walk. If a long straight skirt has slits to allow for walking room, make sure they are modest in length. Also, be aware of skirts and pants cut low on the hips. Some are extreme and are not modest.

Remember, you're not going to walk around like a wooden soldier—you're going to be bending, reaching, moving all the time. Don't buy clothing that reveals a part of your body that shouldn't be showing whether you're standing, sitting or in motion. Now for the final part of the test: look at yourself wearing the article and ask, "Would Heavenly Father be proud of me in this outfit?" If you think He would, then buy it. If there's any question, don't.

This applies to swimming suits, also. Some young women who otherwise dress modestly forget all about modesty when it comes to buying a swimming suit. There are modest suits. In fact, they are the first to sell when swimming suits first come into the stores each year. Shop early. Buy one that covers your stomach and your behind, and comes up high enough on top and low enough on the bottom to be considered modest. Try it on and ask the question, "Would Heavenly Father be proud of me in this swimming suit?"

THERE ARE GOOD REASONS FOR MODESTY

President Faust reminds young women of another reason to be modest. He said, "When strong young priesthood holders see a girl immodestly dressed, most will not want to date her because her standards are not consistent with their eternal perspective. Immodesty in women cheapens their image. It causes embarrassment and loss of respect. It is not likely to win them the hand of a worthy, honorable young man who desires to marry a righteous young woman in the temple."[45]

Can You Sell Yourself Short by the Way You Dress?

Tom, a good looking twenty-six-year-old returned missionary is one example of this. He began dating a young Latter-day Saint woman with the hopes that he might find a wife. They went out a few times and he liked many things about her, but then he stopped dating her. When we asked him why, he said, "I liked her a lot. The problem was she wears low-cut dresses that show too much. I've worked all my life to stay morally clean and worthy of a temple marriage and I don't like the thoughts I get when she wears those clothes. I can't risk being tempted like that, so I broke it off." Later Tom met a lovely young woman who dressed modesty and lived the standards of the Church. His dream came true and they fell in love and were married in the temple.

Should You Listen to Your Brothers?

Julie, a sixteen-year-old young woman, was fortunate. She had two older brothers who cared about her very much. They watched her closely. One day she came out of her room to attend a school activity and was wearing a long-sleeved sheer blouse with a knit tank top underneath. One of her brother's said, "You're not going to wear that, are you?" She said she was, and he said, "No you're not." She said, "Why not? The tank top makes it so nothing really shows." The other brother said, "Believe us, you don't want to know what an outfit like that makes boys think. Now go change into something modest." Julie knew her brothers loved her, so she made the change. As you can see, brothers can be a powerful influence for good.

MODESTY FOR MEN

Modesty isn't just for women. Men must be aware of their dress and appearance, too. The Church leaders have said, "Young men should also maintain modesty in their appearance. All should avoid extremes in clothing, [and] appearance . . ."[46] President Faust said, "Wearing sloppy clothes and weird hairstyles to supposedly look trendy is not proper for one who holds the divine commission of the priesthood."[47]

One extreme we have seen is in the pants some young men wear. They are so big and sloppy that two grandmas could fit inside one pair. Some are so low slung on the hips that the only thing holding them up is the prayers of their mothers. These young men need to bend over and look in the mirror, too. They might be quite shocked to see that the line that divides the east and the west is in plain sight. The Lord can't be pleased with this kind of dress on His young men. Nor would he be pleased with pants that are too tight. Can you picture Jesus wearing clothes like this? He would maintain His dignity and would not want to attract attention by wearing extreme fashions.

Keep Your Shirt On

A young woman told of how her date was so caught up with his mighty muscles that he took his shirt off and flexed them to impress her. That's not appropriate. Even in professional sports, the players wear shirts. An exception, of course, is swimming. When people refer to someone who lost a lot of money they often say, "He lost his shirt." We suggest here that you don't go around looking like a financial pauper. Keep your shirt on. *Your* body is sacred, too.

Encourage Each Other

You young men play another important role in what girls wear. Unfortunately, sometimes men encourage immodesty in women when they whistle or make flattering comments about girls who are immodestly dressed. That sends a powerful message. Good girls who may be wavering in their faith, may believe that they need to dress that way to win the boys' approval. The Lord is not pleased with any young man who would do this. Elder M. Russell Ballard said, "Let the women in your life know that you want them to be women of God and not women of the world. Of you the Lord expects protection and safety for His daughters."[48]

You hold His holy priesthood and he expects you to honor womanhood—always. President Hinckley reminds us of how important this is by quoting a wise saying, "He that governeth himself is greater than he that taketh a city."[49] Men must be sure that they govern their actions and, by so doing, encourage modesty in women.

Young men and young women, you must remember that you are trying to protect your sexual purity and the purity of your friends and associates. What you wear and what you encourage others to wear matters. President Hinckley said, "We must not, we cannot sink to the evils of the world . . . You and I must walk on a higher plane. It may not be easy, but we can do it."[50] Safeguard your virtue by dressing modestly.

Safeguard #6

Get the Angels On Your Side

"For he shall give his angels charge over thee, to keep thee in all thy ways."
–PSALM 91:11

Angels are a very real presence in our lives. We can't see them, but they are there. We can't even imagine how much loving support and help we receive from the spirit world. Elder Neal A. Maxwell promised us that if "we have faith in God and faith in His commandments, His angels will be 'round about [us] to bear [us] up' and 'have charge over [us]'."[51] Angels can play an integral part in keeping us safe from harm and evil in many different ways.

THEY CARE ABOUT US

A faithful Latter-day Saint man told of an experience he had when he had been wrongfully blamed for the misdeeds of another. The mistake came about by his name being forged on legal papers. He didn't know who was responsible for forging his name and didn't know what to do. This good man had lived an honorable life and felt terrible about his reputation being ruined by someone else's wrong doing.

Family Connections Through the Veil

As he was praying and pondering his situation, his departed father visited him and gave him the name of the man responsible. With this information he was able to get his name cleared. The visit from his father was brief, and unmistakably showed the love and concern he had for his son. Who is better suited to help us than those departed loved ones who sincerely care about our welfare? What a sacred responsibility to live worthy of their presence, and what a comfort, as further illustrated in the following examples.

Susan, a woman who was suffering from a serious illness, asked her husband to give her a priesthood blessing. During the blessing he said, "Your grandmother is here watching over you." Her grandmother had died several years prior to this blessing. Susan, who deeply loved her grandmother, was comforted knowing that, at this very moment, she was with her.

Another example was told by Ray, who as a teenager was in a situation that could have compromised his moral standards. All the teenagers at a party were pairing off and disappearing. A very attractive girl was after him to go with her. Ray was about to make a terrible mistake, but he hesitated. At that moment, the spirit of his deceased brother, Arlo, who had died before Ray was even born, spoke to Ray's mind and warned him to leave the party immediately. Tears came to Ray's eyes—he felt Arlo's presence, knew he loved him and was right there trying to help him. Ray left the party, and saved himself from the consequences of a serious moral transgression.

Testimonies of Early Saints

We read of many accounts during the early days of the Church when angels were seen. One of these was during the dedication of the Kirtland Temple. Those present testified that the temple was filled with angels. It was a glorious experience for those early Saints who were present; a heavenly confirmation for them as the Church was being established on earth once again.

Usually angels are not seen, but their presence can sometimes be undeniably felt as Ray felt Arlo's presence. As the pioneer saints crossed the plains, angels assisted them in a variety of ways. President Faust shared the testimony of one of the members of the Martin handcart company, who suffered almost beyond his ability to endure. He said, "I have pulled my handcart when I was so weak and weary from illness and lack of food that I could hardly put one foot ahead of the other. I have gone on [to some point I thought I could never reach, only to feel that] the cart began pushing me. I have looked back many times to see who was pushing my cart, but my eyes saw no one. I knew then that the angels of God were there."[52]

WHEN DO ANGELS COME?

In an *Ensign* article, Elder Bruce C. Hafen posed the question, "When do the angels come?" Then he answered, "If we seek to be worthy, they are near us when we need them most."[53] And one of the most important reasons you could ever need them would be to help guard your sexual purity.

Angelic Rescue

Shellie, a faithful young Latter-day Saint woman who had moved to a city away from home to work, discovered how this can happen. She was frightened to be away from home for the first time and prayed daily for the Lord to protect her and help her. She shared an apartment with two roommates who were asleep in another room the night this incident happened. After Shellie had said her prayers, climbed into her bed, and fallen asleep, she was abruptly awakened. A man was on top of her with a knife at her throat, saying, "Don't scream or I'll kill you." There was no question that he was there to rape her.

Through a power beyond her own, she was able to maintain her composure. She looked him directly in the eyes and said, "God will not let you hurt me. Get out of here right now." He was shocked and said, "If you'll let go of my arm I'll leave." She had not realized that she was holding his arm with a powerful force beyond her own strength. She said, "I knew that angels were helping me." She let go and he ran out the door. She called the police, gave a description, and the man was caught.

That night angels were present, giving Shellie the backup she needed. She received that help because of her righteous living and her faith and prayers. Just as Elder Hafen promised, "If we seek to be worthy, [angels] are near us when we need them most."

Agency, Spiritual Preparation, and God's Ultimate Love

Maybe there are some reading this who have been raped and wonder why they didn't receive the same protection Shellie did. Sometimes bad things happen to very good people and we don't understand why. Heavenly help is always there for the faithful, but it comes in different ways. Sometimes the help comes in strengthening us to endure terrible trials and feel God's presence helping us through them. Sometimes it comes in warnings that help us avoid the trial, such as a possible rape. And sometimes it comes in the form of spiritual power and the assistance of heavenly beings in the moment, such as Shellie received. Sometimes it is there to usher righteous people peacefully through the veil when evil people take their lives. Our job is to prepare spiritually as best we can, and trust God from there.

You might ask yourself this a question: What heavenly assistance would be there for me if I am aware that this help *is* available and ask for it? In the New Testament it is written, "Ye have not because ye ask not" (James 4:2). Shellie had fervently asked Heavenly Father for protection every night, then lived faithfully and received it. Everyone has the right to that same protection. Although God will not usually take away agency from those who determine to do wrong deeds, he often opens a way of escape, or is able to get through to the mind and hearts of those intent on evil deeds to convince them to make a different choice.

Regarding faith that can bring about this type of action we refer to a statement by President Boyd K. Packer. He said, "It is the kind of faith that moves people. It is the kind of faith that sometimes moves things. . . . It is marvelous, even a transcendent power, a power as real and as invisible as electricity. Directed and channeled, it has great effect."[54]

Angels are around us and want to help us. At times we need to open the doors of heaven through our faith and allow the angels to go into action in our behalf, according to God's will.

"They That Be with Us are More"

The story of Elisha in the Bible gives an inspiring account of his experience with angels. The army of the enemy had surrounded this city by night with horses and chariots. The servant of Elisha arose, saw their predicament, went to Elisha, and said, "Alas my master! how shall we do? And he answered, Fear not; for they that be with us are more than they that be with them. And Elisha prayed and said, Lord, I pray thee, open his eyes that he may see. And the Lord opened the eyes of the young man; and he saw: and, behold, the mountain was full of horses and chariots of fire round about Elisha" (2 Kings 6:15-17).

You don't know how many angels are "round about" you, to help you with your battles. Just knowing that angels are present can be a tremendous influence in helping you stay morally clean. How will you behave on a date if you know your departed grandmother, or some other loved one who has passed on, is in the car watching over you? Picture her pleading with you to get away from the temptations; wanting to literally pick you up and carry you away from the evils that could occur. Think seriously about this possibility should you find yourself in a compromising situation. Even ask yourself, "Would my departed loved ones be pleased with what I am doing right now?"

Agency is Always There

A young man had confessed his sin of immorality to his bishop and said, "I knew better, but I just couldn't stop." The bishop said, "Do you mean to tell me that if your mother walked into the room you couldn't stop?"

He quickly answered, "Of course I could stop if that happened."

"Then you still have your agency," said his bishop.

Keep in mind that it may not be your mother who walks in, but it could well be an angel. Think of that and you certainly will have the power to stop anything that could lead to a violation of your sexual purity.

Angels—even mothers—powerfully influence us in different ways. Christy tells of an experience she had. Her mother had diligently taught her about protecting her moral purity. She was very specific in her instructions to Christy. Many times she had stressed that she must never let her guard down. She said, "If you do, the remorse you'll feel after will erase any pleasure you had at the moment. It will never be worth it." She also reminded her that "if you are immoral you can never tell your children of the joy it is to have stayed morally clean. Your example will be powerful in teaching them."

"It Will Never Be Worth It"

When Christy went away to college she went on a concert trip with the school band. The students were asked to stay with friends or relatives in the area where they would be performing. One of their stops was in the town where her boyfriend, Kurt, lived. She hadn't seen him for a couple of months and was looking forward to being with him again. She called his parents and they invited her to stay in their home the night of the concert. She accepted their offer.

That night when she and Kurt arrived home, his parents were in bed asleep in their room on the first floor. Kurt's room and the guest room were upstairs. Kurt showed Christy to her room and explained that his room was next to hers. They kissed goodnight and he went on to his room. A few minutes later she heard a light knock on her door. She opened it and there was Kurt. He said, "We've been apart for so long and I've really missed you. We won't see each other again for a long time. Come and sleep with me. No one will ever know."

She hesitated for just a moment, and during that moment she saw behind and above Kurt's head, her mother's face as though it were on a movie screen. She said, "It was amazing to me how many of my mother's teachings about chastity flashed through my mind when I saw her face. I particularly remember hearing her say, 'It will never be worth it'."

She looked at Kurt and said, "No. I could never do that. Goodnight." She shut the door and has been so very thankful ever since. A few months later she met a wonderful returned missionary in one of her classes and married him in the temple a year later. Just as her mother promised, she had no regrets and she has had the sweet opportunity of teaching her own children of the joy that comes from living morally clean.

THE PART YOU PLAY

It's worth every effort on your part to live worthy of divine help from the spirit world. We suggest three important things you can do to help make this happen.

1. *Pray.* Pray specifically and fervently, morning and night, asking Heavenly Father to protect

you and help you live morally clean. In the Book of Mormon the Savior admonished us to "watch and pray always, lest ye be tempted by the devil, and ye be led away captive by him" (3 Nephi 18:15). In a latter-day scripture He revealed to Joseph Smith that we must "pray always, that you may come off conqueror; yea, that you may conquer Satan, and that you may escape the hands of the servants of Satan that do uphold his work" (D&C 10:5).

Sixteen-year-old Melany told her bishop during an interview that she prayed every day for the Lord to help her stay morally clean. She said, "I want a temple marriage and I know I need His help. I know He loves me and will know what to do to help me stay worthy, if I ask." She also said she prayed for the Lord to help her future husband, whom she had not yet met, to stay morally clean, too.

The prayers of your parents can be a mighty force in protecting you, also. Lois, the mother of three teenage children, said she prays daily for angels to be sent to watch over her children and help them resist the temptations of the devil. Listen to the prayers of your parents as they pray in your family prayers and you will hear them pleading to the Lord in your behalf. You need to know that in addition to these prayers, they are offering many private ones throughout the day—just for you.

President Hinckley tells of a young man in military service. "He was the only Latter-day Saint in his barracks, and he soon wearied of the jibes of his associates. One day when the going was particularly rough, he finally agreed to go into town with the crowd. But as they entered the town, there came before his minds's eye a picture. He saw the kitchen of his home. It was supper time. There was his family, kneeling at the kitchen chairs—his father, mother, two sisters, and a small brother. The little brother was praying, and he was asking our Heavenly Father to look after his brother in the military.

"That mental picture did it. The young man turned away from the crowd. The prayer of that little brother, of that family, brought clarity of mind and courage to the Latter-day Saint youth."[55] Many have lost their virtue in situations like this, but not this young man, because of prayer. Angels were watching over him that day. Through your own prayers and the prayers of those who love you, you too will receive the help you need to live a worthy life. President Hinckley said, "You don't have to be a genius to pray. He will listen to the voice of the most humble."[56]

2. *Read Your Scriptures.* It is a commandment from the Lord and He is pleased with you when you follow this commandment. He knows you will be strengthened by doing so. In urging us to read the scriptures, President Hinckley said, "Let the Lord speak for himself to you, and his words will come as a quiet conviction that will make the words of his critics meaningless."[57] A prophet of God is making it clear that the words of those who try to persuade you to do anything that leads to immorality will be meaningless to you, because you have read the scriptures and know the truth.

Some years ago when I was writing an article about chastity I wanted to interview a young man to discover what it was that helped him stay morally clean. In order to find one who truly had, I asked our bishop if he could recommend someone. He didn't hesitate and directed me to an eighteen-year-old young man by the name of Jeff.

In the interview Jeff said he had watched his dad and knew of the love he had for the Book of Mormon. The family read from the Book of Mormon often, and many times he saw his dad reading it privately. He wanted to have a strong testimony like his father.

When he was fourteen Jeff decided that if he was going to be like his dad, he needed to do what his dad was doing, so he started reading the Book of Mormon every night before going to sleep. He said, "As I did this I started to gain a testimony of the Savior and began to understand what He had done for me. The realization of His sacrifice for me was overwhelming. That's when I knew I would live a morally clean life. I could never hurt Him after all He has done for me."

3. *Listen to the whisperings of the Spirit.* When you were confirmed a member of the Church you were given the gift of the Holy Ghost. You were promised that he would be with you as long as you were trying to live right. If you want to hear his promptings you must be in tune. Wherever you are, if you have a feeling come over you that you should or should not do something, follow

that feeling. The Holy Ghost speaks to us through our feelings. Sometimes he has actually spoken out loud, but that's a rare occurrence. Mostly it just comes as a feeling, or like words spoken quietly in your mind.

Sharon had such an experience when she was on a date. The captain of the debate team, Jim, asked her to go with him to a school dance. Jim was one of the popular guys at school and she was very excited about this date. The couple they went with were in the front seat of the car and Sharon and Jim were in the back seat. As they were driving along after the dance to get something to eat, Jim moved over close to Sharon and put his arm around her. She scooted away, and he moved closer, obviously intending to kiss her. The prompting came that she should tell him to take her home right now. It was an awkward situation because they were with another couple. The feeling was very strong, so she moved his arm away and courageously said to him, "Take me home right now."

Jim was startled by her reaction and said, "What did you say?" She repeated, "Take me home right now." He said, "Well, you're no fun." He told the driver to take her home. As soon as they arrived she jumped out of the car and ran into the house. She found out later that Jim took pride in "scoring" with his dates. He had been immoral with other girls and then bragged about it. He had nothing to brag about with this one, and there were two witnesses to confirm it didn't happen. (Another good reason to double date.)

By following the promptings of the Holy Ghost, Sharon was protected. You, too, can have this constant protection. Sadly, some young women are becoming the aggressive ones and are trying to tempt young men into immoral behavior. The heavens must weep to see this happening. Young men must be on guard and take action as bold as Joseph in the Old Testament did. When Potiphar's wife tried to seduce him he ran from her and any temptation that might have persuaded him otherwise (Genesis 39).

Young men and young women need to listen for the whisperings of the Spirit and follow these protective promptings. The gift of the Holy Ghost has been given to you, in the Savior's own words, "that ye may stand spotless before me at the last day" (3 Nephi 27:20).

As you do these three things—pray, read the scriptures, and listen to the Holy Ghost—you demonstrate your loyalty to Christ. When you take these actions, Satan loses his power over you. You will then be led to do many other things that will help you live a chaste life. You'll want to go to church, serve in your callings, and repent of any transgressions.

These actions empower the angels to act in your behalf. The Prophet Joseph Smith said, "If you live up to your privileges, the angels cannot be restrained from being your associates."[58]

Mission

Marriage

Family

Safeguard #7

Take A Look Into The Future

"Where there is no vision the people perish."
–PROVERBS 29:18

It doesn't take a crystal ball to look into the future, it just takes a little imagination. There *is* a future out there and you are going to play a vitally important role in it, because it's *your* future. Some young people get discouraged because of all the bad things that are happening in the world today, and they get the idea that the world is coming to an end, so why make any plans. If that's your way of thinking, you've just put a big smile on Satan's face. He would love to have you think that, because then he has a greater chance of convincing you to "eat, drink, and be merry, for tomorrow you die." He doesn't want you to be excited about your future and he certainly doesn't want you to prepare for it. He would also want you to think that there is no eternal future. He's absolutely wrong on both counts. You have a great future ahead here on this earth, and the possibility of a glorious future in the eternities to come.

YOU LIVE IN EXCITING TIMES

First, let's discuss your future here in mortality. You live in the most wonderful time of the earth's history. Though evil is all around us and accepted by many who are blinded by Satan's cunning ways, the work of the Lord is rolling forth with mighty power as never before. Always remember that Heavenly Father and Jesus Christ are far more powerful than the devil. Just look at a few things happening within the Church right now:

- New members are joining the Church at an accelerated rate, making the Church the fastest growing religion of our time—remember, the Lord said the gospel would "roll forth, until it has filled the whole earth" (D&C 65:2). It's happening.

• The Church is being recognized and praised in the media as never before. How can the media avoid noticing—Latter-day Saints are a huge force for good that can no longer be ignored.

• The faithful are more faithful than they've ever been. They attend seminary and institute classes, they have family home evening, they help others, they go to the temple, they serve missions, they follow the prophet, and they stand up with courage to those who would drag them down, and they do it with dignity and honor.

• Temples are being built throughout the world at an unprecedented pace to bless the lives of these faithful saints.

• Revelations are coming in a steady and increasing stream from God to our living prophets to prepare, protect, and guide us through these times.

Indeed, it is a wondrous time to be alive, and the future grows brighter and brighter for those who hold to the iron rod of truth.

Visualize Your Future Family

It's important for you to picture yourself in all of the wonderful things that are happening and what role you will be playing as you step onto the stage of your future. Close your eyes for a minute and put on your imaginary "I can see me in the future" glasses. Now take a thirty-year leap ahead. You are married and your children are growing up. It's family home evening and you and your spouse have gathered your children together to help strengthen their testimonies of Christ. You look into their faces, and are filled with an almost overwhelming love for them. Can you see them? They have your smile, your hair, or your eyes. Let them be real in your mind right now. Your oldest daughter just turned sixteen; she's a lovely girl, and you adore her. She can hardly wait for her first date. Young men, would you want her to date someone like you?

Look at your son, young women. He's a good boy and you are so proud of him. Would you want him to date someone like you? We hope you are living a life now that would allow your answer to be a resounding "Yes!"

A young woman told us that it helps her to picture her future children in the spirit world. She said, "It's almost like I can see them looking down at me and saying, 'Please do what's right, Mom. We're pulling for you.'" They *are* up there and you can be sure they're hoping with all their might that you will choose well so they can be born to parents who are pure and faithful.

Be a Righteous Influence on Each Other

Still wearing your imaginary glasses, see yourself as an older teenager. You're talking with one of your friends, a young man who is wavering in his decision to serve a mission. Do you have any idea how important your encouragement is? Doug was a young man who had planned on serving a mission since he was a little boy. He was raised that way and even had a pretty good sum in his mission savings account. However, when he turned eighteen he lost sight of his goal. Some of his friends were not interested in missions and were encouraging him in other directions. One day, as his mother was talking to him about going on a mission, he angrily said, "Don't talk to me about a mission any more!" She was crushed, but she and his father honored his request. They didn't bring it up to him any more, but they did bring it up every night to the Lord. They prayed that someone would help him make the right choice.

Not long after that Doug met Patti, a lovely, faithful Latter-day Saint young woman. They dated for awhile and began to fall in love. When the idea of marriage came up, she said, "I could never marry a man who didn't serve a mission."

He replied, "Oh, I've always wanted to serve a mission."

She said, "Good. I'll write to you every week and pray for you. I'm sure you'll be a good missionary."

During that year before he left they dated, had a wonderful time, and lived morally clean and worthy of temple recommends. He went on his mission and served with honor. She was a powerful influence in helping him choose to serve a mission.

You may be wondering if she waited for him. Actually, she met another young man, a returned missionary, and they were married in the temple about six months before Doug returned home. His parents were concerned about him. When his girlfriend wrote him with the news, he wrote home and said, "It's okay. We prayed about it before I left and both of us had the feeling that we'd marry someone else. She was important in my life at the time and I'll always be grateful for her. There's someone else for me and I'll find her when I come home." He did, and he married her in the temple a year later, and has always been thankful for Patti's influence and how she helped him live worthy of the wonderful blessings he now enjoys.

Sometimes missionaries *do* marry the girl who waited and gave them loving support throughout their missions. If you read the book or see the movie *The Other Side of Heaven,* Elder John H. Groberg's inspiring mission story, you'll see a beautiful example of this. You'll also see how Elder Groberg's love for the Savior and his knowledge of the purity of his girlfriend protected him from temptation when a young woman in the mission field tried to persuade him to be immoral. The influence you have on each other's future is immeasurable.

Project Yourselves Into the Future

In all of your friendships, remember *there is a future out there.* It may help if you young men could see yourselves some future day, sitting in the bishop's office preparing for an interview. Only this time, *you* are the bishop. (Don't laugh—this could happen. Your bishop right now used to be a young man much like you.) Into your office comes a woman you used to date many years ago, seeking a temple recommend. How are you going to feel as you look into her eyes and ask the questions the Lord expects you to ask—questions about her moral purity? Will you be embarrassed because of what you did with her when you were young? Or will you be able to look into her eyes with a conscience clear of any past wrong doing? We hope it's the latter. Carefully consider the possibility that you will one day meet people in unusual circumstances that you knew well when you were younger. Don't burden your future with immoral transgressions today.

Speaking to the youth at General Conference, Elder Harold G. Hillam said, "You and the millions like you, if you prepare well, will be the faithful mothers and fathers in the Church and the Lord's future leaders . . . You will probably want to look in the mirror periodically and remind yourselves of the great mission that lies before you."[59] What a good idea—look in the mirror and let your eyes penetrate to your very soul and give yourself a good interview, much like a bishop would. Be honest with yourself. This will never replace a bishop's interview, but it certainly will prepare you for one, and will help you evaluate how you're doing along the way.

THE BLESSING OF REPENTANCE

This leads to an important principle that has everything to do with your future: *repentance*. President Hinckley said, "If any of you has stepped over the line, please do not think all is lost. The Lord reaches out to help you and there are many willing hands in the church also who will help. Put evil behind you. Pray about the situation, talk with your parents if you can, and talk with your bishop. You will find that he will listen and do so with confidentiality. He will help you . . . Your lives are ahead, and they can be filled with happiness, even though the past may have been marred by sin."[60] He then reminded us that the Lord made this promise to those who repent: "Though your sins be as scarlet, they shall be as white as snow; though they be red like crimson, they shall be as wool" (Isaiah 1:18).

X-Ray of the Soul

To help those seeking forgiveness, a stake president came up with the following analogy. Repentance is like healing a broken bone. When a bone is broken, we must first understand the severity of the break by looking at the damaged area with X-ray to discover where and how it is broken. Then the bone must be put back in place and held there by a strong protective cover to keep it from further damage. This protecting armor holds the bone intact until it heals and becomes strong again.

To repent, we must recognize our mistakes by looking deeply into our acts, and how they have affected us, much like an X-ray, and then make the necessary changes to fix it. We must completely stop the things we are doing wrong, to avoid causing further damage. Then, we must shield ourselves from the temptation while we heal. This is done by talking through our problems with the Lord, our bishop, and, if possible, our parents. We must stay away from the place or situation that caused the problem in the first place. Doing these things provides us with a protective armor which helps keep us from the sin until we become strong again and able to resist the temptation.

No Sin Without Suffering

To help youth understand the seriousness of sin and the depth of repentance required, Elder M. Russell Ballard reported the following: "Recently I talked with several groups of young men and women in Utah and Idaho. They told me that some of our youth feel that they can be immoral during their teen years and then repent when they decide to go on a mission or be married in the temple. Some young men talk about a mission as a time when they will be forgiven from their past sins. They have the notion that a few transgressions now are no big deal because they can repent quickly, go on a mission, and then live happily ever after. . . . please believe me when I tell you that this scenario is a gross deception by Satan; it is a fairy tale. Sin will always, *always,* result in suffering. It may come sooner, or it may come later, but it will come."[61]

A mission president told us that sometimes missionaries don't fully confess their sins until they are on their missions and finally realize how important it is for their own eternal salvation. He said, "It's very difficult for a missionary if his unconfessed sins involved sexual immorality. He may have to be sent home to complete the repentance process, and that's very hard on him. He or she needs to repent *completely* before coming on the mission, not just 'sort of' repent."

President Hinckley confirmed that "This is the time, this is the very hour, to repent of any evil in the past, to ask for forgiveness, to stand a little taller and then go forward with confidence and faith."[62]

The Truth About Repentance

A faithful young mother told us her story of repentance with the hope that it would help others.

As a teenager she stopped living the standards of the Church because she became confused when her parents divorced. She dated boys who were not members of the Church and fell into the trap of immoral living. She was miserable, but didn't relate her misery to her immorality. She thought living the "free" life would bring her happiness. It brought the opposite—sorrow and depression. One day she heard a song that reminded her of the Church and the teachings she had left behind. She said, "A wonderful, peaceful feeling came over me as I heard that song, and it made me remember why I came to earth and what I must do to be happy." She returned to church, met with her bishop, repented and got her life back in order. A couple of years later, as a worthy young woman, she met and fell in love with a worthy young man and they were married in the temple. She has expressed her gratitude for repentance over and over, and has remained faithful in the Church. But she wishes with all her heart that she had lived her life so that she never had to repent of immoral acts.

President Hinckley said, "[Virtue] is the only way to freedom from regret. The peace of conscience which flows therefrom is the only personal peace that is not counterfeit."[63] Refraining from doing wrong is the best way, but for all who have sinned, repenting now will pave the way to a much happier road in the future.

REMEMBER WHY YOU'RE HERE

Remembering why you came to earth can have a significant influence in helping you live morally clean. It's good to reflect back to the beginning, when you were in the spirit world before your birth. You were a valiant follower of Heavenly Father and Jesus Christ. You wanted to come to earth to gain a body and to prove to your Father that you would keep His commandments and live worthy to return to Him one day. And now here you are! What a wondrous opportunity it is to be on this earth experiencing your second estate and preparing for your third estate in the Celestial Kingdom. Knowing where you came from and why you are here helps you understand why it's so important to focus on where you're going. Sister Sheri Dew, former counselor in the General Relief Society Presidency, said, "The voice of the Spirit . . . reveals to us our identity, which isn't just who we are, but who we have always been. . . . *Noble* and *great. Courageous* and *determined. Faithful* and *fearless.* That's who you are."[64]

You have always been sons and daughters of a Father in Heaven who loves you—before you were born, now and forever after. President Ezra Taft Benson sets the record straight about who you *really* are: "While our generation will be comparable in wickedness to the days of Noah, when the Lord cleansed the earth by flood, there is a major difference this time. It is that God has saved for the final inning some of His strongest children, who will help bear off the kingdom triumphantly."[65]

That's you! Wow! What a privilege to be one of "His strongest children." Whatever the temptations are, because of *who you are* and *who you have always been* you can make it. Not only will you make it, you will make it "triumphantly." There is definitely a future out there—prepare for it and live for it.

Spiritual Preparation Keeps Us Steadfast

Pres. Hinckley said, "This is the great day of preparation in your lives, so that as the years pass you will remain steadfast and true and be happy."[66]

Even though trials come—and they do, even to the faithful—you can still be happy, if, as the prophet says, you "remain steadfast and true." There will be trials and troubles in your future; it's part of the plan, it's mortality. Going through tough times allows your faith to be tested, and through the exercise of that faith you will become stronger. Through trials we learn to turn to God and our love for Him increases. By keeping the commandments we qualify ourselves for His divine help.

Looking at Trials with a Godly Perspective

A couple we know faced a challenge they never dreamed would be theirs. They were faithful in the Church, married in the temple and went forth with their plans for a family. One of their children was born with serious mental and physical handicaps, and another with challenging learning disabilities. These parents' hearts were broken. They had hoped and prayed for healthy children and wanted each one of them to be able to enjoy a happy and productive life.

During this difficult time someone said to them, "You must be angry with God for what he has done to you." Their reply was, "Oh, no. How could we be angry with Him—He's the one who is helping us through it. He has guided us and our dear children in remarkable ways. And we can never thank Him enough for them and for all the love and help He has given us." This couple also understands the Lord's plan of salvation and how all things are justified in the eternities. They said, "This life is just a small part of our existence. We will see these children with perfect minds and bodies in the next life, and because of the sealing power of the temple, we'll be together experiencing a joy we can't yet begin to comprehend. That knowledge brings us a lot of happiness now."

That's how it works. When you do your best to live your life true to the faith, repenting when needed, and go on with trust in the Lord, He blesses you and you *are* happy, even in the midst of challenges.

Choosing How to Respond

Sometimes people do terrible things to children that makes it more difficult for them to find happiness as they're growing up. At times these tragic things lead them to an immoral life in their youth. Always remember that, no matter what happens to you, you are still in control of how you will let that affect your future.

A woman told us of her trial when she was a child. Her father left the family and never returned. She yearned to see him and be loved by him. She tells of the many times she would sit at the window, watching and hoping that he would drive down their lane and come home. It never happened. Besides that, her mother was a harsh woman who treated her with disdain. Praise was something this little girl never received. She said, "All I got from my mother was criticism and insults that hurt worse than a beating." This is a lovely Latter-day Saint woman who is married to a wonderful man and has children of her own now who love her dearly. She is known by her associates as one who gives love and kindness to all.

We asked her how it was that she is able to do this after being raised in such an abusive environment. She said, "Whenever I was being abused by my mother or anyone else I would always say this silent prayer: 'Father, please bless me that I will never treat others the way I am being treated right now.' Heavenly Father has answered my prayer and filled me with love for others." She said she never compromised her standards, never succumbed to immoral relationships to compensate for the love she didn't receive at home. She lived faithful to the Lord so that she could one day enjoy the sweet love of her own future family. With Heavenly Father's help, she did it and so can anyone else who may have experienced abuse or heartache.

If experiences you've had have caused you to feel anger and resentment, ask the Lord to cleanse them from your heart. If you have been tempted into committing sin and used your mistreatment as justification, repent and accept the full responsibility of your own choices. We do not have to choose to be less than faithful because of other people's poor choices. Be faithful and the Lord will reward and guide you. Give the gift of faith and purity to your future husband or wife and it will mean everything to your future family. Nothing is more precious than that.

YOUR FUTURE MATE

The choice regarding who you marry is one of the most important choices you will make in this life. Elder Gerald N. Lund said the following after being called as a General Authority. "When I was sixteen years old and not smart enough to know very much at all, the Spirit touched my heart and I realized the significance of the woman that you marry. And starting at that time I began to pray that the Lord would find for me the woman that would be an eternal companion. Those prayers were answered and all that we now enjoy in our family with children and grandchildren is largely [because of] her."[67] Choosing a mate requires your most careful consideration and preparation.

This is not a decision to be feared, but simply to be lived for and prayed about. Do not expect to marry a perfect person—there are none, except

Jesus, and He's not in the running. But there are wonderful people out there who are on the road to perfection. *Be one* and *find one,* then work together to make a loving, faithful family. Heavenly Father will guide you in this vitally important decision if you ask for His help.

YOUR PATRIARCHAL BLESSING

To discover some of the blessings the Lord has in store for you in the future, you can receive a patriarchal blessing from your stake patriarch. You must be morally clean and faithful in the Church to be worthy. Those of you who have your patriarchal blessing, read it often and let it be a guide and comfort to you. If you don't have one yet, talk to your parents and bishop about it.

President Benson gave this counsel: "I would encourage you . . . to receive a patriarchal blessing. Study it carefully and regard it as personal scripture to you—for that is what it is. A patriarchal blessing is the inspired and prophetic statement of your life's mission together with blessings, cautions, and admonitions as the patriarch may be prompted to give."[68]

Some people make a small copy of their patriarchal blessing, laminate it and carry it with them. This is a good idea because you will have it with you to read when you are away on vacation, or at work, or in any situation where you may need to be fortified. It will help you remember the Lord's plan for you now and in the eternities.

Elder LeGrand Richards assured us that, "If we understand where we came from, why we are here, and where we are going, then we are more likely to reach the desired port."[69] That "desired port" is worth all the effort.

MAKE YOUR DECISION

Decide today that you are going to be morally clean and worthy to enter the temple. Put a picture of your favorite temple on your bedroom wall. Look at it every day and let it remind you of your goal. Then pray each morning and night, asking Heavenly Father to help you reach that goal. Always remember that you are His daughter or son, and you are going to live worthy to return to Him one day.

There is a future out there—here on earth and in the eternities—and it's filled with hope and happiness for you and for all who live God's moral laws and keep His commandments. He has revealed that "Eye hath not seen, nor ear heard, neither have entered into the heart of man, the things which God hath prepared for them that love him" (1 Corinthians 2:9).

What a glorious future awaits you!

NOTES

[1] Ezra Taft Benson, *Ensign,* Nov. 1986, p. 83

[2] *For the Strength of Youth* (The Church of Jesus Christ of Latter-day Saints, 2001) p. 26

[3] Richard G. Scott, *Ensign,* Nov. 1994, p. 37

[4] Gordon B. Hinckley, *Ensign,* May 1996, p. 91

[5] *Teachings of Gordon B. Hinckley* (Deseret Book, Salt Lake City, UT 1997) pp. 720, 721

[6] Pam Stenzel, *Finding True Love,* Pro-Life America Web Site, pro-life.com

[7] Neal A. Maxwell, "What Is Real Love and Happiness?" *New Era* June 1992, p.4

[8] *Sexually Transmitted Disease Surveillance 2000,* Department of Health and Human Service, Center for Disease Control and Prevention, Atlanta, GA, p. 41

[9] *Encyclopedia of Mormonism* (Macmillan Publishing Company, New York, 1992) p. 7 and Boyd K. Packer, "Covenants" *Ensign* Nov. 1990, p. 85)

[10] Deborah Cardomone, Pro-Life America, Redondo Beach, CA

[11] Ibid.

[12] Pam Stengel, *Finding True Love*

[13] Bishops Handbook (The Church of Jesus Christ of Latter-day Saints)

[14] Larry L. Bumpass, James A. Sweet, and Andrew Cherlin, "The Role of Cohabitation in Declining Rates of Marriage," *Journal of Marriage and the Family,* Vol. 53, 1991, pp. 913-927

[15] CT Inc. Research Department, *Christianity Today Marriage and Divorce Survey Report,* July, 1992

[16] Karen Stinneford, *Embracing Chastity,* Winston-Salem Journal, Feb. 13, 1994, p. E3

[17] President Gordon B. Hinckley, "A Prophets Counsel and Prayer for Youth," *New Era,* Jan. 2001, p. 4

[18] Spencer W. Kimball, *The Miracle of Forgiveness* (Salt Lake City, UT: Bookcraft, 1969) pp 241-42

[19] *For the Strength of Youth,* p. 12

[20] Gordon B. Hinckley, *New Era,* Jan. 2001, p. 4

[21] Ibid

[22] Spencer W. Kimball, *The Teachings of Spencer W. Kimball,* Edited by Edward L. Kimball, Salt Lake City, UT, Bookcraft, 1982, Chapter 10

[23] Spencer W. Kimball, *The Miracle of Forgiveness*

[24] Ibid, p 66

[25] Ibid, p 66

[26] Ibid. pp 77-78

[27] Thomas S. Monson, *Church News,* April 6, 2002, p. 3

[28] M. Russell Ballard, "Purity Precedes Power," *Ensign,* Nov. 1990, p. 35

[29] *Webster's New World Dictionary,* Second Edition (Prentice-Hall, Englewood Cliffs, NJ, 1970,) pp 1351 and 1584

[30] Gordon B. Hinckley, *Ensign,* May 1996, p. 91

[31] Ezra Taft Benson, "To the Youth of the Noble Birthright," *Ensign,* May 1986

[32] Keith Merrill, "The Enemy Among Us," *Meridian,* meridianmagazine.com, March, 2002

[33] Gordon B. Hinckley, *Ensign,* Nov. 1997, p. 51

[34] Gordon B. Hinckley, BYU devotional, Provo, UT, 17 Oct. 1995

[35] *Teachings of Gordon B. Hinckley,* p. 463

[36] Jeffrey R. Holland, "Sanctify Yourselves," *Ensign,* Nov 2000, p. 39

[37] Gordon B. Hinckley, *Ensign,* May 1998

[38] Ezra Taft Benson, Ibid

[39] William R. Bradford, Conference Report, Apr. 1976, p. 146

[40] Gordon B. Hinckley, *Ensign,* May 1996, p. 92

[41] David O. McKay, *Gospel Ideals,* p. 352

[42] *The Kansas City Star,* Apr 17, 2001.

[43] James E. Faust, "Womanhood: The Highest Place of Honor," *Ensign,* May 2000, p. 95

[44] Jacque Truman, "Modesty Las Vegas Style," *Desert Saints* magazine, March 2002, p. 21

[45] Ibid

[46] *For the Strength of Youth,* p. 16

[47] James E. Faust, "The Power of Self-Mastery," *Ensign,* May 2000, p. 43

[48] M. Russell Ballard, "Women of Righteousness," *Ensign,* April 2002, p. 69

[49] *Teachings of Gordon B. Hinckley,* p. 378

[50] Gordon B. Hinckley, *Stand a Little Taller* (Salt Lake City, UT: Deseret Book, 2001) p. 34

[51] Neal A. Maxwell, *Ensign,* Nov. 2001, p. 80, and D&C 84:88, 109:22

[52] James E. Faust, *Ensign,* May 1979, p. 53

[53] Bruce C. Hafen, *Ensign,* April 1992, p. 16

[54] Boyd K. Packer, *Faith* (Salt Lake City, UT: Deseret Book, 1983) p. 43

[55] *Teachings of Gordon B. Hinckley,* pp. 467, 468

[56] Ibid, p. 469

[57] Ibid, p. 572

[58] Quoted by President James E. Faust, *Ensign,* May 2998, p. 97

[59] Harold G. Hillam, "Future Leaders," *Ensign,* May 2000, p. 10

[60] Gordon B. Hinckley, "Stand True and Faithful," *Ensign,* May 1996, p. 94

[61] M. Russell Ballard, "Purity Precedes Power," *Ensign,* Nov. 1990, p. 35

[62] Gordon B. Hinckley, "Stand True and Faithful," *Ensign,* May 1996, p. 94

[63] Ibid, p. 379

[64] Sheri Dew, *No Doubt About It* (Salt Lake City, UT: Bookcraft, 2001) p. 36, 42

[65] Ezra Taft Benson, *The Teachings of Ezra Taft Benson* (Salt Lake City, UT: Bookcraft, 1988) p. 104

[66] *Teachings of Gordon B. Hinckley,* p. 471

[67] Gerald N. Lund, General Conference talk, April 7, 2002

[68] Ezra Taft Benson, *Ensign,* May 1986, pp. 43-44)

[69] LeGrand Richards, "Patriarchal Blessings," *New Era,* Feb. 1977, p. 4

INDEX

For Your Notes

On Guard!

Seven Safeguards to Protect Your Sexual Purity

"I absolutely love this book! It's amazing and powerful! The safeguards are simple yet can have such an incredible influence on my life now and eternally. Thank you!"

–**Rachel, 17,** high school senior

"It's a marvelous book! And badly needed."

–**Janice Kapp Perry,** songwriter

"On Guard! *is a must read for every teenager, young adult, bishop, church leader and parent. It's filled with wonderful quotes of the brethren, touching stories and do-able ideas that have the power to change behavior and inspire temple worthiness."*

–**Ed J. Pinegar,** Institute of Religion teacher, speaker, co-author of *Leadership for Saints*

"I am so impressed with this book. I wish this could be required reading for everyone in the Church."

–**Darla Isackson,** editor, author, mother of 5 sons

Gary and Joy Lundberg are also authors of the best-selling books on relationships, *I Don't Have to Make Everything All Better* and *Married for Better, Not Worse*. Gary is a marriage and family therapist and singer. Joy is a writer, poet and songwriter. They present seminars and firesides throughout the U.S. as well as teach classes for CES. They live in Provo, Utah and are parents of five children. For more about their books and music visit their Web site at **www.allbetter.net.**

ISBN: 0-915029-05-7

50695

9 780915 029051

Riverpark Publishing
Provo, Utah
801-224-3447